Why Smart Girls

Get into

Bad Relationships

And How Not To Do It Again

Barbara Leigh

Light Switch ON Books, LLC

P.O. Box 375
West Bend, WI 53095
262-247-6643

LightSwitchONBooks.com

First Edition

Edited by Carol Shay Hornung and Kathy Hayevsky
Proofread by Veronica Hoffman

Library of Congress Control Number 2024912878
ISBN 979-8-9907724-0-3 (paperback)
ISBN 979-8-9907724-2-7 (hardcover)
ISBN 979-8-9907724-1-0 (ebook)

To Angela – You asked for it.

To Kyle – You made it better for everyone else.

And to Tiffany – You saw the vision.

Contents

Introduction

Most of the ideas in this book will benefit people without regard to gender. However, a lot of books on bad relationships do not get into social oppression of women and how that affects the way they enter and try to find their place in relationships. Hence, it becomes "smart girls" and not "smart people." I do try to use inclusive language throughout, as most of the content is not specific to women. If you are part of another socially oppressed group, feel free to substitute or add your specific examples to the belief #3 section in Chapter 2.

In Chapter 3, Step 3, I use examples of societal attitudes toward men. I want to make clear that these are not examples of social oppression because they are conveying power, not removing power. Oppression removes power. These examples are specific to men who *do not want* the power being conveyed onto them. There is a difference. Again, you can substitute in whatever examples apply to the person in power in your type(s) of social oppression.

That said, I believe the concepts in this book are useful for anyone who feels they have lost the real version of themselves—however that happened. I want to focus on relationships here and use familiar examples. Not all females feel the effects of social oppression. That's not my story and I'm not going to presume to know yours. My hope is that you can still find something useful in my experience.

Chapter One
The Map

Why "smart girls" you ask? You don't have to currently believe you are a "smart girl" in order to benefit from this book. If you have spent any amount of time in your life as a female and felt you could trust yourself to make good decisions at some point, you may relate to the emotional identity of the "smart girl." This identity and its belief system is a good part of how I ended up at the end of a relationship with zero self-esteem, blinking and completely at a loss. I wondered how I got here. I felt like I had no idea where things went off the rails. This was a bit unnerving. I'm smart! I should be able to figure this out! But then it got absolutely terrifying. If I couldn't see it, if I didn't recognize it, then *I will do the same thing again*. That was totally unacceptable.

And that's where I decided to search for the answers to my questions. I've been on a journey of many years of self-reflection, research, therapy, discussions with people along the way, eye-opening discoveries, plenty of setbacks and painful revelations, lots of aha! moments and, always, hope. This book is my effort to share what I found to help you rebuild and find the confidence to move forward, knowing you won't be in that lost and terrifying place again.

I like to look at it as a map—not everything is spelled out for you because your situation is your own. You will most likely run into some bad weather and detours along the way. This book can give you some direction and help you visualize where you are going, but it's your own journey.

Part I covers some beliefs I had about me and how they were twisted into being used against me.

The Beliefs

1. I can trust myself.
2. I am a good, helpful person.
3. I am smart, but I can't appear smarter than my partner.
4. I must guard my relationship, not only from outside, but from inside too.
5. It is important to keep things steady and stable.
6. Self-care is indulgent and not a priority.
7. I have emotional muscle and I can muscle through anything.
8. I can rely on my smartness to figure it out.
9. Partial is enough. I can (and should) fill in the rest.

It's not that I ever really thought about these beliefs; they just were my reality. They were modeled by my parents or my grandparents or my greater community. They were indirectly taught in my religious education and in school. You learn the message that rings most true with what you know, whether it was intended or not. These are mine; they may not be yours. Your beliefs may include thoughts like, "I am not safe" or "I can't trust anyone but me." The plan is to find a way to rewrite your beliefs, whatever they may be, to make them healthier for you and to keep you from ending up in the same spot over and over again.

The beliefs may seem normal, reasonable even. But when applied in a relationship, they can turn against you.

How the beliefs turn into bad relationships

1. *See beliefs #1-2; You are a leader; insecure people are attracted to leaders.*
2. *See belief #3; You tone yourself down to allow your partner to lead.*
3. *Your partner doesn't want to lead, isn't good at it, feels shamed, and reacts poorly.*
4. *You are betraying yourself. You feel shame and respond poorly.*
5. *See beliefs #4-9. You try to fix it.*
6. *Your partner blames you for changing; you are not the person you were before.*
7. *Relationship implodes.*

The part that makes it a bad relationship is the fact that, at the end of it, you have zero self-esteem. A relationship that leaves you there is just bad. Whatever it was that sucked the life out of you: emotional, verbal, physical and/or sexual abuse, a narcissistic partner, mental health issues, or just giving too much of yourself without getting anything in return; whatever it was, it removed you from you.

Once you find yourself there, it's time to grieve, build yourself back up, reassess and learn the skills it takes not to repeat this cycle. Part II covers this process. Grieving is a very real part of the process and skipping it isn't an option. It involves a reset of the body, mind and soul. You are choosing to survive. It's an opportunity to stop and evaluate what you're going to bring forward and what you will leave behind, what has worked and what has not. If you are further out from the relationship but find yourself reading this book, chances are you got stuck somewhere in the grieving process. The goal is to provide skills that will get you moving forward again.

As part of your evaluation, you will likely find that your beliefs may seem reasonable, but they aren't working and need revision. Chapter 5 will take a look at some common beliefs and why they may not be working. In the same way most people with any driving experience believe they are the best driver on the road, there are things we can choose to be a little more realistic about. There are other things we were told that simply aren't true. Learning to recognize truth is a big part of revising your beliefs. We'll also cover the reasons stable and secure are not always in your best interest when reviewing your beliefs.

Chapter 6 goes into the effect the stress of the bad relationship has on you physically. Your body has been working really hard to keep you from harm and, as a result, it has depleted supplies of things you need to flourish and created stockpiles of things that a healthy body shouldn't need. You're physically out of balance. We'll look at some ways you can help your body now and tools you can use to keep the balance going forward.

You are worth more than survival.

To heal, you will have to choose yourself and decide you are worth the work. Like in the grieving process above, where you choose to survive, at some point you need to become aware that you are doing this because you are worth it. You are worth getting out of bed every day, moving your body, doing the work of sifting through all of the feelings, digging through the beliefs and continuing to move forward. You are worth more than survival. Chapter 7 will go into how to build up the self-esteem that was lost and find your value.

It's likely that you have lost or disconnected from your support system. You will need to do what it takes to reconnect or find a new one. It's vital that you don't do this alone. People need people; it's that simple. Beyond that, you need the perspective of other people. When you question a situation, having someone to give a second opinion is priceless. Not that every decision should be reviewed, but when you're having a weird feeling about something, there's nothing like a fresh perspective to clear up uncertainty. It's interesting how listening to someone else gives you a new angle on your own situation. You may find you need professional help as well, and I encourage you to go that route in addition to building your personal network. The more perspectives you have, the clearer the full picture of your life becomes.

All of the above will help when you get to the difficult process of rewriting your beliefs and actually believing the new ones. It's that "actually believing them" that really gets you. Even though you have gone through the process and rooted out the truth and found your value, it's hard to let go of those messages you've been hearing your whole life. Know that your hard work has paid off, and you may not notice it right away, but you will find yourself recognizing the old beliefs as they come up. Once you recognize them, you can more easily reject them as old and not useful anymore. You can leave them at the edge of your new boundary and no longer let them define you. You can move on to see yourself on a much larger scale, in tune with the universe and your purpose there, rather than being defined by those around you.

Even if the relationship ended a long time ago, it's never too late to go through this process. If you look at your life and feel stuck, that's a good indication that there is some work to be done and the real You inside would like to move forward now, please and thank you. The hope is that when you get through the process, you can start to once again trust yourself, and that's what Part III addresses. It doesn't happen all at once and it isn't magic, but you will start to see the truth where lies once were. You will know your value. You will think of yourself as whole.

As you heal, you will no doubt have new perspectives on old problems. You will come up with more feelings to work through. You will have triggering moments that will bring you back to feeling like square one. But you will take the skills you have learned and use them to get you through the difficult moments. You will be able to see the positive and work toward it. And you will move forward again, knowing you can get there and this setback is only temporary.

Only you can know what moving on looks like for you. You will make goals and have dreams. You will move forward. When you look toward your future with confidence and without fear, fully being yourself and knowing your truth, that's when you know you've moved on.

If your life brings you someone new, coming into a budding relationship as a whole person is the best gift you could give that person. Knowing your truth, recognizing your value, and living with confidence may feel familiar, but there will be a whole lot of knowledge behind it that wasn't there before. Communicating who you are, where you've been and where your boundaries are will be part of building that relationship. Looking for that honesty in your partner will help establish that they too are a whole person. Finding someone that is willing to recognize the hard spots and to work through them rather than run from them will allow you to set aside your fears and proceed with confidence. That kind of confidence is based on a new belief for your list, *"I will not betray who I am."*

Part I: Smart Girl Beliefs and the Self-Destructive Results

Chapter Two
The Beliefs

I wanted to know what it was about me that made this bad relationship possible. I was pretty sure I knew what it was about my partner, and I was fine with putting the blame there, but that's not something I can change, and I needed to learn how to avoid the problem next time. It happened once, that's more than enough. What was it about me that led me here?

The Beliefs
1. *I can trust myself.*
2. *I am a good, helpful person.*
3. *I am smart, but I can't appear smarter than my partner.*
4. *I must guard my relationship, not only from outside, but from inside too.*
5. *It is important to keep things steady and stable.*
6. *Self-care is indulgent and not a priority.*

7. *I have emotional muscle and I can muscle through anything.*

8. *I can rely on my smartness to figure it out.*

9. *Partial is enough. I can (and should) fill in the rest.*

Going deeper, I wanted to know more specifically where these beliefs came from. At what point did my brain learn these ideas?

1. I can trust myself. As a small child, I was quick to learn. As I grew, I started making decisions and most of them were good ones. I trusted my instincts and the things I had learned, and applied them to new situations. Most of the time everything turned out alright and I felt like I was capable and trustworthy.

2. I am a good, helpful person. This one is reinforced from many directions.

- Religion—the woman was "created to be the helpmate," help the poor, the widow, the sick, etc.
- School—being helpful is rewarded.
- Society—in farming communities like the one I grew up in, helping each other is survival.
- Family—helping your family members and being a caregiver is expected.
- Youth Organizations—whether it's 4-H, Scouts, mission trips, or whatever city kids do, your goal quite often involves helping someone.
- Work—helping your team, your customer, your mission.

I'm sure there are more, but you get the point. Helping is a core value in our society, and for good reason. People don't do well alone. We all need help at some point. Our society depends on people helping each other to continue to exist. In order to keep our communities healthy, we instill and reinforce a strong need to be helpful within its members.

3. I am smart, but I can't appear smarter than my partner. Now we start getting deep into girl territory. You learn early on that males and females are different and societal expectations differ for each.

- As a child, you probably did not have toys or books that portrayed positive, non-stereotyped heroes that were female. Male superheroes are generally fully dressed, albeit in spandex.
- You were taught that your wardrobe can get you sexually assaulted and know that, in many eyes, it would be *your fault*. Typical males generally do not think about getting sexually assaulted based on what they wear in public.
- When violence happens to men it is called crime. When it happens to women it is called "domestic violence" or "date rape" and is treated with less importance and/or disbelief.
- You likely have planned your movement through public spaces in order to avoid being sexually harassed. It generally doesn't occur to males to think about that.
- If you are sexually active, you have a good chance of being labeled a "slut," but males who are sexually active are "studs."

By the time you are a teenager, the above expectations have taught you that boys/men aren't able to control themselves and that *girls/women are responsible for the actions of males*. Not only are girls/women responsible for male actions, but we also *need a male* and should attract one using deception and exploitation of our bodies. Marketing has given us a long list of messages.

- You are expected to "take care of yourself," meaning look attractive, often through extraordinary and expensive means.
- When you turn on the TV, watch a movie or open a newspaper, you see few women represented in ways that are not sexualized.
- According to these images, you can't be feminine AND strong.
- Women are encouraged to hate their bodies. Just type that sentence into a search engine to find the myriad of ways this happens.

But we feel like we can't be "too much" because society has led us to believe that it will cause us to lose the male. The points below suggest that *females have less worth than males* and reinforces that we need a male to handle important things. It doesn't matter if we're good at them or not, men are simply assumed to be better. When women function outside of expected behaviors, they are often told they are "too much" and men will feel threatened by them.

- Though movies are getting better about portraying women as capable, they can still give us the feeling we need a man to make us complete.
- Poor financial decisions are attributed to your gender.
- The expectation is women are poor negotiators.
- Driving mistakes are attributed to your gender.

- You are not capable of making your own medical decisions.
- Your general ability is questioned depending on the time of the month.
- Your lived experience is most likely that mom does the most repetitive and unrewarding chores, if not most of the household work. Mom probably also made any needed career sacrifices for the family.

It's possible that every female has a different version of how social oppression affects their beliefs. I see hints of it in my beliefs #4-9. You may find it elsewhere but, for me, it jumps front and center in belief #3. You may have no problem appearing smarter than your partner but there's some other area where you refuse to be "more than" your partner. Many Christian women have been told they aren't allowed to lead a man. My version happens to be about not hurting their pride, which I think started from a well-intentioned place. Added to the above, it ends up being more harmful than intended.

All of these are messages that we see and hear over and over again every day. If you are part of another socially oppressed group, you may want to make a list of your own lived experiences. These experiences are reinforced in the media we consume, in our working lives, what we see when we go shopping and to events, and in our homes. We may even spew them at other people because they become so ingrained in our thinking that they become true to us. Whether we believe them consciously or not, these influences show up in how we treat ourselves and others. When we start appearing smarter (or in some way better) than our significant other, we may feel the need to not be *too much*, to give them the focus, or to assume the supporting role.

Back to not hurting their pride. On top of all of the above, I am a people pleaser. Maybe it's because my older siblings hated me as a child. Maybe it was because I could never please my mother by being the extrovert she wanted me to be, since I very much was not. In any case, I really wanted to help people, so I watched them. I could tell by the smallest details in their reactions how what I said affected them. I would do whatever I could to save them from distress, whether a family member or a stranger on the street. My grandma once insinuated that by dating a certain person, I could help them get on, or stay on, "the right path." My people-pleasing self grabbed that and ran, so it became, "as a female, I should shelter my partner from any negative emotions that they might have."

There are other reasons for sheltering your partner. You may have had an abusive or unstable parent that you needed to tiptoe around in order to feel safe. You may have grown up in a situation of neglect where your needs weren't met and you needed to be the caregiver. You may be a very emotionally-driven person who feels other peoples' emotions as strongly as their own. It may have nothing to do with being female. But for me, using my "womanly wiles" was part of this idea of being able to influence my partner, for better or for worse.

* * *

The rest of the belief list (#4-9) consists of codependent behaviors learned as a family dynamic, an interpretation of religious belief, part of the societal expectations of females, a system devised to help handle a situation and protect ourselves, or a combo platter of all that and more. For me, it was learned from several places, including my family. My mom could be screaming full tilt at my dad but, if the phone rang, she could turn on a dime and answer with her sweetest voice. We did not discuss our troubles, or even let people know we had any.

Codependency encompasses a whole bunch of behaviors that boil down to *not letting the people you love receive the consequences of their own actions.* You wear yourself out trying to control all aspects of the messy people in your life. You feel like the person spinning plates at the circus. You don't want to allow the people, the relationships, or the details of your life or theirs to fail. You get so hyper-focused on making it all work, keeping the plates spinning, that you lose sight of whether it's good for you, or for the people you are trying to "fix."

Your list may vary, but you'll likely pick up these themes in how your codependent behaviors impact your relationships with yourself and others. This list is representative, not comprehensive.

Codependency encompasses ... not letting the people you love receive the consequences of their own actions.

---

4. **I must guard my relationship, not only from outside, but from inside too.** As a female, I was conditioned to feel responsible for the actions of the male in my life. I would try to make him look good and control what our life together looked like. I didn't want other people judging me, my choices, or our

relationship. I chose to wear a mask to conceal the failure I felt because the harder I tried, the worse it got. It never occurred to me to talk to or get advice from someone on the outside about my relationship problems because, in my experience, that wasn't a thing we did. These choices isolated me from friends and family.

Trying to save him from his own consequences only allowed him to push further down the path of unhealthy behavior for himself and for our relationship. I tried to be perfect. I would register all of his complaints about me, take responsibility for them, and try to do better. That seemed like a healthy thing to do. The problem was, the complaints were not real. They were a (successful) attempt to manipulate and control me. I was measuring my worth against what he told me he valued, and I was coming up sorely lacking, which was his (probably subconscious) intent. Not that he was intentionally wanting me to feel inferior, he just didn't want the disappointment of our relationship to be his fault or have anything to do with him. Instead of choosing myself and seeing that I wasn't being valued for who I was, I chose to guard the relationship by denying myself and becoming someone else who tried to control all of the things.

5. It is important to keep things steady and stable. Rather than setting healthy boundaries, I chose not to fight for what I believed in, or what I wanted or needed. It was more important to stay steady than to have my needs met. It was more important to meet the needs of my partner to keep things calm. I *turned off my feelings* so I wouldn't rock the boat. I didn't know it at the time, but that was a critical point in my bad relationship.

6. Self-care is indulgent and not a priority. Somewhere along the way, I got so caught up in the business of taking care of others that I stopped taking care of myself. Not that I "let myself go" (as in not taking care of my outward appearance) because that would involve allowing the outside world to see my chaos. I stopped asking for my needs to be met and put off things that would keep my mind and body healthy. At that point, my self-esteem hit an all-time low and I felt that everyone and everything else was more worthy of attention than me. I stopped doing things that involved creativity and self-expression. If there was a thought, it was "I shouldn't need to [care for myself], I'll figure it out."

7. I have emotional muscle and I can muscle through anything. I was in a wildly dysfunctional relationship. All of my energy was spent trying to control my partner's aggression toward me. I chose not to see the cycle and felt instead like I was working toward some mystery destination that I could get to if I worked hard enough at it, as if at any moment there would be a magical realization that I am worthy of love and all of the chaos would be gone. The goal was to hang on and wait for that moment. Surprise, that's not how it works. The issue isn't you or your worth, so there will be no magic moment. The issue has everything to do with your partner's emotional and mental health and history. No amount of emotional muscle on your part is going to fix that. Unfortunately, when you start out thinking everyone is mentally healthy and you are going to have a normal, healthy relationship, it's hard to recognize and embrace the fact that what you have instead is dysfunction. Your emotional muscle may be amazing, but you need to train it to hold on to that which is healthy for you. I did not.

8. I can rely on my smartness to figure it out. I had always depended on my smartness to get through tough situations. I didn't want to admit that this was more than I could figure out. Denial, embarrassment, fear of failure, and fear of the unknown kept me from moving forward. And then there was the codependent part of this belief that being smart enough made me responsible for taking care of other people who weren't as likely to figure it out. But I also assumed that other people saw the world the same way I did. My smartness didn't account for the different perspectives and experiences that other people brought to the situation unless, of course, I knew their experience and was able to calculate that into my assessment. I was never going to understand my partner because he didn't *actually* think like me and neither of us was willing or able to talk about it. My assumption that he was coming from my perspective made it much harder to grasp his aggression toward me, and much easier to accept the blame for it.

Selfless is fine for a one-off heroic act, but not as a way of life.

---

9. Partial is enough, I can (and should) fill in the rest. I tried to create a "whole" relationship by filling in all the gaps. At first, I asked for what I needed. When I was told no, I made excuses. As time went on, I stopped asking for what I needed and eventually stopped believing that I was worthy of having it. Then I decided I didn't need it, so there were no longer gaps. What I couldn't give up, I did for myself. It didn't occur to me at that point that this was not okay, or that healthy relationships involve give and take from both partners. I was doing what I was supposed to do. I was being a good, helpful person. I was trying to put my partner first. I was guarding my relationship, keeping it stable. I didn't worry about what this was doing to me. Wasn't being selfless what I was supposed to be doing?!? What I was actually doing was being codependent. Needed does not equal loved. Selflessness is fine for a one-off heroic act, but not as a way of life. Without your sense of self, you are unable to have healthy relationships, which starts this whole cycle again, and why we need to address "how not to do it again."

Chapter Three
The Results

How to Tank a Relationship in 7 Easy Steps

1. See beliefs #1-2; You are a leader; insecure people are attracted to leaders.
2. See belief #3; You tone yourself down to allow your partner to lead.
3. Your partner doesn't want to lead, isn't good at it, feels shamed, and reacts poorly.
4. You are betraying yourself. You feel shame and respond poorly.
5. See beliefs #4-9. You try to fix it.
6. Your partner blames you for changing; you are not the person you were before.
7. Relationship implodes.

Step 1: See beliefs #1-2; You are a leader; insecure people are attracted to leaders.

When you are smart and you trust yourself, leading is easy. Whether you want to lead or not, people just naturally follow you. And I'm not talking about "on social media." People value your opinion and you see the responsibility in that.

Sometimes potential partners are threatened by your strength which may make you feel lonely or untouchable. You try to be the good, helpful person you are *supposed* to be. The people around you love to be treated well. You feel good about yourself. At some point, someone pursues you because that is the person you are. You will lead and you will be good to them and help them. Being pursued is a nice change. They aren't afraid of you and seem to need you. You start a relationship and, at first, you are both happy with the arrangement and it seems to work really well.

Here we need to touch on the insecure person for a moment. According to Brené Brown in her book *Atlas of the Heart*, there's a difference between "interpersonal insecurity" and "personal insecurity." While the first is about how we handle relationships with others – being unsure about incoming love and trust and our own worth in relation to others – the second is about our relationship with ourselves and being unsure about measuring up to what we think we *should* be. She points out that people who think highly of themselves can *still be insecure* if they don't think they are measuring up to some inner gauge of worth.

Brown also discusses research on the opposite state, that of being "self-secure," and how people who aren't so critical of themselves tend to have qualities that make them more successful in relationships with others.[1] Looking at that from my perspective, it seems that insecurity may be hard to spot if you don't know what you're looking for. The insecure person is uncertain about core relationship foundations and doesn't really know what healthy relationship behaviors look like. They feel like they don't measure up, so it is hard for them to accept love, or trust someone else to find them worthy of love. This does not make them a bad person, but it does set them up for a lot of doubts and fears. How they handle those doubts and fears is often destructive to their relationships. This is how we get to step #2.

Step 2: See belief #3; You tone yourself down to allow your partner to lead.

At some point, your beliefs start poking through. You pick up on their need for you and translate that into your own version of what that means. The voices that carry your beliefs echo in your head: "You're too much," "You need to be supportive," "You need to keep things calm." While those voices rattle around in your subconscious, you start hearing messages from your partner: "You're not enough." "You made me do that." "It's your fault."

Your truth screams to be heard over the noise. Rather than heed your own truth, you bury it in desperate attempts to fix the quickly snowballing issues. You try to provide the security your partner lacks by stepping back, by allowing them onto your stage, by giving them your voice. You internalize the lies coming

---

[1] Brené Brown, Ph.D., MSW, *Atlas of the Heart: Mapping Meaningful Connection and the Language of Human Experience* (New York: Random House, 2021), 173-174.

from your partner and from your beliefs, and you make yourself less than Who You Are.

Step 3: Your partner doesn't want to lead, isn't good at it, feels shamed, and reacts poorly.

Your partner does not welcome your retreat. What drew them to you was your strength and ability to lead them. They needed you to fill what was missing in them, the security they desperately wanted, and they don't see security in being a leader. They feel shame and fear. If your partner is male, he has all the conditioning of being told he should "be the man" and "head of the family" on top of the fact that he doesn't want to lead and is not good at it. We've already established that this person is prone to a lot of doubts and fears and is not comfortable with their own weaknesses. Your withdrawal highlights their weakness. This does not go well for your relationship.

Step 4: You are betraying yourself, feel shame and respond poorly.

At this point, you are starting to lose yourself. You've abandoned your own truth and made yourself "less than" to save your relationship and it only seems to be getting worse. You no longer feel like you can trust yourself and you're starting to question whether you are a good person. You feel shame and self-doubt. The expectation that your partner would think and respond the way you would was unfounded, and that realization leaves you off balance. You make yourself smaller and smaller.

When you hit this point, you find you've turned off your emotions rather than feel. The part of you that makes you feel alive has been given to someone who doesn't want it. It leaves you out of touch with Who You Are. You do everything you can to lift up your partner, to elevate them to lead, to be who they want you to be. It just terrifies them. Your partner says, "you are not enough" and you believe them because you are doing everything you know how to do, and it is clearly not enough. It is easy to believe that it is your fault. The person who once pursued you turns against you. Shame becomes your constant companion. This does not go well for your relationship.

Step 5: See beliefs #4-9. You try to fix it.

You try to fix the relationship by going back to your core beliefs. You cycle through, trying to find something that will help. These are truths, right? You are trying to get some truth back into your relationship but, unfortunately, your beliefs aren't actually true. They are codependent behaviors that keep you in a cycle of fear and shame. You keep accepting the blame for your partner's choices while trying to shield them from their own consequences, all while denying the things that make you Who You Are.

Step 6: Your partner blames you for changing; you are not the person you were before.

Your partner blames you for changing. They wanted the confident person you were; they didn't want to lead. They don't know how to be vulnerable enough to have the conversations needed to tell you what they do or do not want, or even to allow themselves to name their own emotions. They end up fearing you and, as that happens, they make you the villain. Every destructive choice they make becomes your fault. You keep accepting the blame and silencing your voice.

Step 7: Relationship implodes.

At some point, you make yourself so small you no longer fit in the box you've stuffed yourself into. You don't recognize who you've become. You keep yourself busy all the time (or use substances and/or addictions) to avoid having to think about it. You may find it easier to avoid your partner altogether.

Your partner becomes fearful to the point of being unstable. They may also use avoidance, keeping busy, addictions, or substances to control their fear. They may lash out at you or engage in behaviors that are designed to spite you. You do everything you can to keep things calm. Somewhere in this mess, a trigger happens and it all goes splat. It may be one or the other or both of you. It may be a huge external explosion or a pop inside that completely changes someone's perspective. In any case, it becomes unsustainable and it has to stop.

It is likely you have been carefully tiptoeing around triggers for a while, and you may still be dodging them. If you are still in the relationship, I am not here to convince you to leave. There are circumstances that make leaving not a viable option. As long as you are strong enough to draw the line between the "old relationship" and the "new relationship," whether that be an agreement between you and your partner, or a line drawn in your own head about what you believe and what you don't, you are still worth it and you can still choose to use this book to heal and move forward. At the least, I hope this book helps you recognize what unsustainable looks like.

If you choose NOT to heal, and you still have zero self-esteem, you are likely to stay in the same place doing the same things, either in this relationship or the next. You may even become the insecure one in another unsustainable situation. If you feel too overwhelmed to begin, please seek professional help. You do not have to do this alone. You have the power to stop the cycle if you make the choice to heal.

* * *

The "bad relationship" removed you from you. All of the things you enjoyed about yourself now seem to be the cause of your failure. It is not your fault. *I repeat, it is not your fault.* You didn't ask to be in a bad relationship. You didn't ask to be belittled or blamed. You did not see the insecurity in your partner, and wouldn't have known how that would affect your relationship if you had. *You did not deserve that.* If you haven't yet, recognize that it is no longer acceptable to be treated in a way that leaves you with zero self-esteem. *You are worthy of being loved and appreciated.* Turn that over in your mind. Embrace it. Let it fill you. Understand that this book points out things that you can watch for and things you can control now that you are here on the other end of the bad relationship, knowing what you know now. Holding yourself responsible for what you didn't know before is not helpful or productive. The rest of this book is designed to help you move from here to a place where you can be You and trust yourself to "not do it again."

Part II: Do the Work to Understand and Rewrite the Beliefs

Chapter Four
Good Grief

Literally, grief is good for your soul. So first, you grieve. Grieving is very important anytime you run into change or loss, not just in relationships. Life is hard, people! The world changes around us all the time. Learn to make grieving part of the way you handle change because it helps provide perspective and enables you to move forward.

Relationships end for a lot of reasons. For me, I was pushed to the point where I finally stopped and recognized, no, I DO NOT deserve to be treated like this. That is a helpful place to be, because it lends you perspective to compare other ways you were treated against what you deserve. That may not be your story. There is an entire spectrum of possibilities. It may have been sudden; it may have been a long, slow decline. You may not have seen the end coming, or you may have run screaming right at it. You may not be at the end yet and are wondering what that looks like. That's okay!

<u>Why should you grieve?</u>

Normally when you think of grief, you think of death and funerals. While that's not what I am talking about, it has its similarities. You expect to be sad and grieve when someone with whom you had a beautiful, loving relationship dies. Whether the person or only the relationship dies, grieving helps you make the transition from who you were in that relationship to a new version of you.

But it's the same when the relationship was more on the ugly side. There's still a transition that needs to take place. It doesn't mean you miss being mistreated. It doesn't mean you liked having no self-esteem. It's allowing yourself to respectfully acknowledge the loss of the person you were, perhaps the more innocent and trusting version of you, and make room for the person you will become. It's not about "losing" your partner, it's about losing the You that you were before or that you had become in that relationship. If the word grief makes you cringe, you are welcome to call it something else, like "phoenix-in-progress." That says, "I'm picking myself up out of this pile of ashes I've become, and I will rise into something even more beautiful than I was before. It's still a process, gonna take some time."

These are some things I've learned about grief:

Allow yourself time to build up your strength, emotionally, mentally, and physically. It takes time and a whole lot of energy to pick yourself up from "the end" and get to a position where you can do what you need to regain trust in yourself. Being able to trust yourself not to do it again is the ultimate goal here. But this building up period is about getting you to a place where your brain and body are functioning enough for you to actually use your smart person skills and learn some new ones. It is a process, and you don't need to rush through it. You do need to keep moving forward, but it can be a creep, a crawl, or step by step. It's not a race. Honor your need to recognize your losses. Value the time you spent, the good there was (or you thought there was), and the lessons learned. I strongly encourage you to take the time to grieve the relationship you thought you had, the version of yourself you were, the plans you had for the relationship, and/or the way life was before the relationship. It doesn't have to be 'real' to be grieved because what we expect, plan for, and hope for are all very real to us. Grieving is a transition, from "who we were" to "who we are" going forward, and both of those states have real goals and dreams.

Honor your need to recognize your losses.

Know that, even if the relationship wasn't good for you, it's still okay and important to feel bad or sad or whatever you're feeling. It is very common to think that since the relationship was bad for us, we're not allowed to feel the feelings we're having. You don't have to grieve the parts that hurt you, but you can if you want to or need to. It doesn't matter whether the feelings are anger and frustration, or if there was some feeling of familiarity that was lost. There may be subconscious reasons you entered this relationship in the first place and exploring those feelings can help you connect the dots as to why you made some of the choices you made. Explore the feelings; allow yourself to feel them fully. You may discover something about yourself by letting those feelings fully develop. If you uncover something in this moment, you can choose to explore it or you can choose to come back to it later when you are stronger. It's a process. Do it at your own pace. All the feelings at once probably won't serve you well. I would caution you to remember that more than one thing led you here. Don't let yourself get hung up on one and stop noticing the rest. You'll need the whole picture to fully heal.

You may have also been denying your feelings so long you no longer feel comfortable having feelings. Have the feelings! Acknowledge not only the existence of the feelings, but the value and range of them. Experience them fully. There are all kinds of losses, or at least changes, involved. Don't downplay their impact. Whatever you feel separated from, or feel you lost, should be grieved. Unacknowledged grief can really mess with your body, mind, and soul.

There's no right way to grieve. If you have heard of the five stages of grief, (denial, anger, bargaining, depression and acceptance), great. In reality, it is not an orderly walk through five steps. It bounces all over the place and revisits everything multiple times. Feel the emotions you need to feel. Everybody does it differently. You're allowed to feel like you're healing one day and be completely sad the next. The main thing is to continue moving through it.

Don't get stuck. It is really easy to get stuck in grief. Recognizing your losses and allowing your mind and soul to process through them is an important part of healing. Let your feelings fully develop. Allow the feeling to enter, meet it, discover the source of it, give yourself permission to feel the emotion even though it may not agree with your beliefs, look at it from different perspectives, learn from it and, when you're ready, let it go and move on. This is different than becoming a seething ball of rage or getting sucked into a black hole of depression, both of which are examples of what getting stuck looks like. I'm not saying this process is easy. Chances are you've been stifling your feelings for a while and this is going to be a completely foreign experience for you.

There is no graduation. You don't "complete" grief. You will hopefully get to a point where the grief is manageable and you can start to work on other things as well. You may still be experiencing grief in some areas, but moving ahead in others.

As you start to explore your beliefs and uncover other areas that need reexamination, you will find more feelings to process, and you may get thrown back to things you thought you had already processed. Don't panic, it's normal and actually quite healthy. It means you are seeing the past from a new perspective and you need to reconcile that view of it with what you already know. You eventually integrate the losses into the new version of You.

* * *

Enough about what it is, I know the burning question is:

How do I do it?!?

Like I said, everybody does it differently, but here are some things I've found to be helpful.

Building yourself up

Take care of your body. Grief can be debilitating. It can steal your ability to function on a physical level. If you're trying to find a way forward from a place of zero self-esteem, or a pile of ash, the first priority is to give your body some attention. This doesn't require complicated thoughts or emotions. It is just straight-up giving your body the things it needs. These acts tell your body, "I am choosing to survive."

- Breathe
- Drink water
- Eat healthy food
- Sleep
- Move

These points may seem obvious, but there have been times where I have needed to make conscious choices to do all of them. I have been so tense I didn't notice I was actually holding my breath. My muscles have been so tight I have pulled my back out. I have been so distracted I haven't remembered to eat or drink. My anxiety has been at such high levels I have gone for days without sleeping. If you have problems with doing these basic things for your body, talk to your doctor. Anxiety medications helped me sleep, a few core exercises from my chiropractor helped loosen up my back. I am here to tell you getting help can be life changing.

Your body was with you in your bad relationship and has adapted to that environment. The brain rewires itself to the pathways it uses most, so don't be surprised that your brain has become a stress ninja and has a hard time relaxing. It can take time for your body to switch gears, but that beautiful body wants you to heal and will do what it can to make that happen. We'll talk more about breathing later but, for now, just get that brain some oxygen. Drinking water helps cleanse the toxic results of all that stress out of your body. Eating natural and whole foods rather than processed foods gives your body more opportunities to heal and replenish the nutrients it needs. Learn to listen to your body and give it the attention it deserves.

Learn some mental health self-help tools. There are many tools you can learn to help pull you back down when you are spiraling out of control. Mental health professionals are trained to give you scads of these specific to your issues. These are a few of my go-to favorites given to me by friends, family, and therapists, but what works for me may not work for you. Ask around about what has worked for others, get some counseling and ask for tools specific to you, or do an online search, typing in something like, "anxiety tools." Warning, that may be more overwhelming and anxiety-inducing, but you get the idea.

- **Grounding techniques for anxiety**—when you're feeling very anxious, pulling yourself back into physical reality helps to ground you. This can be as simple as putting your hand on your leg, feeling the cloth or the skin, and noticing the textures or temperature. If it's hard to focus enough to do that, try walking through the Five Senses Exercise. This is more structured and will require more of your attention, which will hopefully reel in your spiraling anxiety. It goes like this:
  - o Name five things you can see
  - o Four things you can touch

- ○ Three things you can hear
- ○ Two things you can smell
- ○ One thing you can taste.
- **Breathe**—there are many ways to do this and, to be honest, I'm not very good at it. Just know that the goal is to pull you out of fight-or-flight mode which makes you breathe in a faster, shallower way, and bring you into relax and refuel mode, which is slower and deeper. Focusing on breathing helps ground your spiraling thoughts by returning your attention to your physical body. I tend to overthink the how-to-breathe part. Sometimes musical training is not helpful.
- **Go outside**—Nature can be very healing. Feel the warmth of the sun or see the glow of the moon. Smell the dirt or grass; touch the rain on your face; taste a snowflake. The largeness of nature pulls your senses into engagement.

Feeling the Feels

Another mental health tool I learned from a friend is designed to help you learn to feel again. When you have turned off your feelings for a long time, me telling you to have the feelings is not terribly helpful. Been there.

Think of a TV show, movie, musical, book, etc. that makes you cry (or want to cry). What is it that you relate to enough to feel? Work with that. You may need to dig pretty deep to find it. Where's the specific thing that hits home? What scene, what specific line or action? Is it the main character that is doing the action or is it some other character? Is it something a character says? Is it something they don't say or do?

Sometimes it's easier to feel our feelings if we disguise them as someone else's feelings. Sometimes we get angry because the character didn't do what we wanted them to do. What did we need them to do, and why? Picking out the triggering situation or character may be obvious, or it may be a complete mystery. Once you start identifying the specifics of where your traps are, you can start naming the feelings attached to them. From there you can start dealing with them and resetting your system. If just thinking about this exercise freaks you out, I would suggest getting the help of a mental health professional to guide you through the process of learning to feel your suppressed emotions.

I don't say this lightly; this is an important step. You will not heal without feeling, but bringing out those feelings can be very traumatic. A good therapist can help you navigate that. I also am being specific because I have not always found therapy beneficial, and it helps to know what you need help with. Going into it with the words, "I would like a therapist who can help me learn to feel emotions I have suppressed," is much clearer than scheduling a random appointment. A clear purpose can get you to someone who has experience dealing with that specific issue. That experience can make all the difference in addressing your needs.

Getting Stuck

Repetitive negative thoughts, rage, and depression are all signs that you've gotten stuck. Other states that may not be as easy to recognize are denial ("It wasn't that bad, I don't have to change anything"), hopelessness ("There's nothing I can do about it"), busyness ("If I keep myself distracted, I won't have to think about it") or victimhood ("It was all them"). Not being able to move forward or not being able to change your thought patterns is a very real trap, and one that requires some skills to work through. Please get help with this process if you feel it's needed. I can give you tips that I've learned, but I am not a professional. I would be thrilled if this book helped you find the words to express where you are stuck.

Repetitive negative thoughts can send you down a long and unproductive rabbit hole. The first thing you need to do is *notice them.* If you've been entertaining negative thoughts for a while, that's not as easy as it sounds, but it is important. Jill Bolte Taylor, Ph.D., neuroanatomist and author of *Whole Brain Living*, describes what physically happens when an emotional response is triggered as the "90 Second Rule." She says the chemistry involved in that emotion takes 90 seconds to complete the cycle of washing through us and out of our bloodstream. That is all! If the trigger stops, it is gone.[2]

More simply, if you encounter something that trips your trigger, you have 90 seconds to attach a positive thought to the emotion. Rather than thinking, "it's all my fault" or "I am in danger," you can choose to think, "their reaction is not my responsibility" or assess the situation and reassure yourself, "I am okay." You could also think of it as waiting it out. Check your watch and wait 90 seconds. Avoid negative thoughts during that time, and try not to allow the situation to re-trigger and start

---

[2.] Jill Bolte Taylor, Ph.D., *Whole Brain Living: The Anatomy of Choice and the Four Characters That Drive Our Life* (Carlsbad, CA: Hay House, Inc.), 7.

the clock over again. I know this sounds way easier than it is. Redirecting when fight-or-flight kicks in is hard. But if this gives you a life ring to reach for, take it. Noticing the negative thoughts is the key to stopping them. Using that emotional muscle in belief #7 (I have emotional muscle and I can muscle through anything) can redirect negative thoughts to positive ones.

Anger is a common grief reaction and can be directed at yourself or others. It is used as a way to feel more in control or to appear stronger. But mostly anger is a mask. Being angry allows you to avoid feeling the complex emotions that surround a loss. If rage and anger are your go-to reaction, take a look at your thought patterns. Is there a specific emotion that triggers your anger? Can you look at it from a different perspective? Can you press pause on the cycle that moves it from the emotion to thought (like the negative thoughts above,) to lashing out, and ask yourself to consider the actual emotion instead? Does it go against your beliefs? Do you need to reassess those beliefs? That's even more change! You may need to unravel a whole web of emotions to get to the cause of your anger. That's okay. Again, this is not a race. You can work on the process as you are able.

Depression is the sadness and apathy for life that you think of when you hear the word, but it's also a disconnection from others. I understand this relationship that robbed you of your self-esteem also likely robbed you of your community. I'm here to tell you there are plenty of others out here like you, and you are not the only one. Please, please, please get professional help if your sadness and apathy are overwhelming. If you are feeling unable or unwilling to connect with anyone, call 988 (in the

U.S.) or a local mental health crisis line, especially if you are having thoughts of harming yourself. You are far too precious to ignore those signs. Don't let a bad relationship steal any more from you than it already has. You can survive this. You are worth it.

Denial is choosing to believe that the loss didn't really happen. In the case of a bad relationship, the "loss" is your self-esteem, self-security, and whatever else this relationship took from you. As females, we have been taught from various sources to deny ourselves. As a result, we tend to downplay the losses. You may still have some truths to sort out about what was your responsibility and what was not. You may need to build up some self-worth before you can move on from denial. You may still be stuck in a codependent cycle of not wanting your partner to feel the consequences of their actions. Give yourself some grace, keep working on processing your feelings and taking care of your body, and eventually you will build up enough self-worth to stop denying what happened. You will see it as real, and as something you don't want to do again.

Hopelessness comes in when we feel like we can't change. You are reading this book for a reason. Just by moving past the cover on this book, you are expressing hope that you can change. By getting this far, you have already read some ideas that will help you make changes. You can do this!

Busyness is my worst enemy. Busyness is an excuse to not do the work. I'm too busy, I can work on Me later. The kids have this thing, work is crazy, I have all these obligations. Again, this comes out of a place where you have been told you are not worthy. Processing your beliefs needs to take more priority. You are worthy and the process will make you a better, less fearful person.

Belief #2 (I am a good, helpful person) is being twisted here. While being good and helpful is a highly encouraged societal belief, our busyness is taking it beyond that to *my value comes from* being a good, helpful person. False. Your value comes from being who you were meant to be, freely you, expressing and creating what only you can do. If part of freely expressing yourself is physically doing things for other people, that's great. Keep doing that. But if it's sucking away your energy, that's probably not freedom.

This is another place where codependency is a real problem. Do you need to be all things for your kids/parents/friends? Are you trying to control the results of their actions (or inactions)? Your relationships are important but so are you, and you need to find that balance. Same with your volunteer positions and/or work obligations. Are you trying to control things that are not yours to control? Does your work/life balance actually have balance? If not, reprioritizing and moving yourself up the list is in order.

I'm not saying you need to work on this 24/7. For example, you may take some time off from processing around the holidays. It can definitely be a buzzkill. If you're still not back to it a month later, there is likely some avoidance involved. Be aware of the traps you set for yourself. Time management skills such as scheduling time to work on you, and breaking the tasks up into smaller pieces (today I will make the list of emotions/situations/ideas that I need to think about, on Saturday I will pick one and go through the process of fleshing it out) can help keep you on track if you are filling your time with other things. Knowing that you are worth it is key.

Victimhood is where you decide it was all your partner's fault and there is nothing you can do differently to avoid the same problem next time. That sounds absolutely terrifying to me, but if you're in that boat, you may want to stop to think about where you are putting your power. The whole point of this book is to help you take back the power you lost to this relationship. I'm assuming you're probably not in this state if you are reading "and how not to do it again" but, in case you were just reading out of curiosity, find your power and take it back. You are worth it.

* * *

All of these ways to get stuck can just be reasonable pauses. If you have not had the time and the energy to build up your strength both physically and emotionally, you will likely end up in at least one of these for a while. That's okay—this is a process. You need to recover. It may take a while to find yourself back. If you can use the above thought traps to explore the thoughts behind the trap and push through it to why you are worth not getting stuck there, all the better. The goal is to believe you are worth it. Once you have that, you should be able to move past these pit stops.

Getting Past Grief

Again, you don't graduate. There's no official end. You hopefully get to a point where you can feel the feelings without them running your life, or where you no longer feel like a pile of raw nerve endings. You can concentrate on other things and may not think about the aspects of your grief/change/transition/phoenix-in-progress for hours or even days at a time. Your life goes on. The process may take you five minutes or fifteen years. You may be tentative about moving forward, or you may have made a plan and feel like it's time to get started! There's no right way to do it. You may leap forward and then find things that you need to go back and deal with because you now understand them from a different angle. That is to be expected.

The rest of Part II will go through some tools that can help you with the process of managing your feelings and moving on. Examining the sources, beliefs and perspectives that come into play leads us to the types of tools we need, why they are helpful, and how we can use them to heal.

Chapter Five
Choose Yourself

Resist the urge to be the victim. Be open to being wrong/vulnerable/uncomfortable. We talked about the origins of the beliefs in Chapter 2. You've heard some of these ideas your whole life. It stands to reason that you would believe them to be true, or that you would interpret other things as true based on how you understood the expectations you grew up with. It never occurred to you that they would be used against you or twisted to mean something harmful to you. But here we are. I'm here to tell you it's real and it happens. It's up to you to decide what parts of your beliefs are wrong. That can be an uncomfortable process. It can also be a liberating process.

To illustrate this point: I had a coworker who became bored with her job. She didn't see the challenge in it anymore. She moved on, got a new job, and was very excited about it. When I checked in with her after several months, she said she still loved it but felt uncomfortable because she didn't know enough yet.

Knowing her history with my employer and seeing her in this position, I told her to embrace the uncomfortable because that's where she shines. And, uncomfortable or not, she *was* shining! Learning and growing and finding your place can be uncomfortable, but uncomfortable doesn't mean bad. Familiar can be bad or good, depending on what you are familiar with. Don't mistake comfortable and familiar for good. It may be the opposite of what you need.

Let's review the beliefs. Again, you can fill in your own. This is a representative list, meant mostly to help you visualize how this works and give you ways to think about your own beliefs. As you review the beliefs, you may notice that your inability to fix the situation while cycling though beliefs 4-9 has left you feeling like belief #1 is wrong.

The Beliefs

1. I can trust myself.
2. I am a good, helpful person.
3. I am smart, but I can't appear smarter than my partner.
4. I must guard my relationship, not only from outside, but from inside.
5. It is important to keep things steady and stable.
6. Self-care is indulgent and not a priority.
7. I have emotional muscle and I can muscle through anything.
8. I can rely on my smartness to figure it out.
9. Partial is enough. I can (and should) fill in the rest.

Looking at the above list from where I stand now, I can see where the beliefs are not always true or helpful. In fact, there are several that contributed to being very hurtful to me. While some are indeed faulty, we can't throw them all out just because some haven't worked out for us.

You are trustworthy. You can still trust yourself. To do that, you need to go back to listening to yourself and you need to find your true Self again. And maybe you actually can't trust yourself *right now*, but please believe you are still in there, because that belief will guide you back to the You that is trustworthy. If you have mental health issues, you will likely need to dig even deeper, or maybe pull up harder, to find your true Self – and it won't be easy.

If you've heard the expression, "the depression lifted," you get a good sense of how some mental health issues work. They are like a big, heavy blanket you put over your emotions when you are unequipped to deal with what happens to you. But down underneath that blanket, or pile of blankets, is still your true Self, safely nested inside. Your Self may be feeling squished by the blankets, and sometimes a person gets smothered by the blankets. You're going to have to fight to get some fresh air under those blankets, fight for the person you know you are. Know there is hope. Whatever it was you were unequipped to handle when it happened can be taken out and dealt with more appropriately when you feel ready to do that. Take the time to build up strength first. It doesn't have to all be done at once. You may just start fluffing the blankets. Maybe you'll throw the top one in the washer to give it a good cleaning. Maybe it doesn't need to go back on the pile after all. Could be it feels better to have it off. There are physical reactions that happen to your brain as a result of trauma or long-term stress. Please know it takes time to reverse those changes and there is no magic, but it can happen.

How do you know when you can trust yourself? You can trust yourself *when you are being honest* with yourself. Being dishonest with ourselves is how we got here, so my plan was, "don't do that." For the most part, that has worked for me. Not because it's great wisdom, but because it gave me a way to measure truth. Does it feel like I used to feel? I don't want it. Does it feel true? I'll go that way. Does it feel hurtful to my Self? Does it build me up? Learning to listen to that inner Self and following what is right for you will guide you to a much healthier relationship with your trustworthy Self.

One way to help you create a list of your own beliefs is to ask yourself, "What do you lie about?" Try thinking along the lines of "little white lies." What do you choose not to tell people? What do you minimize? What do you straight-up lie about? Why? What are you trying to protect? What are you trying to avoid? Why do you choose lies over truth in that situation? What do you gain?

In my case, I discovered my goal was not to hurt anyone's feelings. That seems innocent enough. I'm protecting them. But when it reinforces bad behavior, it can have consequences. For example, when my partner would be overly friendly with someone who was clearly uncomfortable, I might lie and say, "I saw something over here that you should see." "You're making everyone uncomfortable here, including me" would have been the truth, but I felt like that was too harsh. Now, I'm sure there's a less offensive way to say it, but in any case, it would have been better to tell him the truth in a constructive way than to avoid or lie about it. Dropping my codependent behavior of trying to control him or clean up after him and letting the natural consequences of the behavior come back to rest on him, not me, would have freed me to be myself. Hindsight being what it is, it would have been better for him to have learned social cues early on than for me to pretend it was okay, make excuses for it, and ultimately watch it spin wildly out of control.

What does that mean about how I lie to myself? My beliefs led to codependent behaviors about sparing people's feelings and trying to control those situations. This can be a window into how lies creep into your beliefs about you. This pattern told me that he wasn't responsible for his behavior, I was. That's a lie.

Fair warning, you may not like what your honest and trustworthy Self is telling you. It may not agree with your religion, politics, family or society in general. It may not agree with things you've been told all your life. I encourage you to hear it anyway. Think about why you believe what you believe. You may want to add some items to your list of beliefs to be evaluated. Maybe the belief itself is fine, but you're interpreting it based on a faulty premise from your past that you can root out.

There is some truth within the list of beliefs. **The trick is to find the truth within** and modify the belief to reflect only truth. If you have childhood trauma, underlying mental health conditions, or if your relationship lasted long enough that you internalized the lies you were told about yourself, there may be beliefs that are completely untrue. Taking the time to build up your strength and to get in touch with your true Self, finding your self-confidence, and learning to trust your own voice again will go a long way toward helping you decipher truth from lies.

When I first hit "the end," I had nothing—no strength, no energy, no self-confidence, and no self-esteem. I made the choice to give myself time to recover. I remained in the relationship, but it was now a completely different dynamic. I didn't automatically believe what I was being told. I considered and rejected statements that didn't ring true. I started seeing the patterns of thoughts and behavior that were harmful to me for what they were.

My list of beliefs then probably would have looked different. I didn't know it at the time, but I was starting to set boundaries for myself. I was choosing what to allow in. And that is how I slowly began to build my self-worth. I chose me. I rejected lies about me. I decided to take care of my body and build up my strength. I chose to see the behaviors for what they were. Most importantly, *I believed that I deserved to be free.*

**Taking the time to build up your strength
and to get in touch with your true Self,
finding your self-confidence,
and learning to trust your own voice again
will go a long way toward helping you
decipher truth from lies.**

It didn't happen overnight. While I can say the realization that I deserved better was a light bulb moment, it took time for me to become strong enough to trust my own choices and live my own life. That's what a bad relationship does—it makes you question yourself so much that you become dependent on it.

Eventually I felt strong enough to be my own person, but that took time and lots of thoughtful choices.

Looking back, I can see that while I was in that relationship, I wasn't able to be the kind of parent, daughter, employee, or any other role that I wanted to be because I wasn't healthy, I wasn't fully present, and I didn't have the energy to invest in anything except trying to control the lives around me.

My main way of handling the situation was to stop feeling. My emotional needs were not being met so I chose to ignore them. I chose the busyness of codependency over feeling. I was being held responsible for "making" my partner feel something or do something, so it made sense to me that I should do what I could to control all of the things. That is a terrible idea, but it does keep you very busy. It also makes you feel like you're doing something productive (though it's not actually helpful), and your busyness helps you avoid thinking about anything for any length of time. You can successfully avoid your emotions for a long time. Did I mention this is not helpful? When I started choosing me, I realized that I was not responsible for my partner's feelings or actions. My value did not come from how well I could control those feelings and actions. I didn't immediately break the habits of codependency, but I did start breaking the thought patterns that got me there.

I keep telling you it's not a race because only you can decide when you are ready to fight for yourself and when you are ready to change your thought patterns. Take each step as you are ready. Trying to rush it can leave you pushing for something you don't yet actually believe or, perhaps, reinforcing a belief that isn't actually true. Even though it isn't a race, there is definitely a goal. No matter the speed, walk forward with intent.

How do you evaluate the truth of your beliefs?

There are all kinds of ways to discover that your beliefs just plain aren't true, or are only partially true. Exploring your feelings about a situation can clue you in to faulty beliefs.

One way to check your beliefs is by paying attention to your body. I found a great example of this while listening to an episode of Glennon Doyle's podcast, "We Can Do Hard Things," with Jen Hatmaker.[3] Jen was discussing intuition vs. anxiety. She checks by listening to her body. What is the body response? Is this coming from a quiet place or a chaotic place? Quiet is more trustworthy. When is it happening? Is it the same the next morning? I thought this was so insightful, partly because I ignored my body for a long time, but also because it is helpful to a) take the time to listen to your body, b) have a system to evaluate it, and c) realize that a body response *may not be trustworthy.*

The question Hatmaker asks about the quiet or chaotic place reminds me of the warnings about phishing emails. Phishing emails want you to act now because it short circuits your common sense. Urgency makes you do things you wouldn't normally do because you don't stop to think. When your body tells you to quit your job, is that coming from your anxiety? Are you agitated and feeling urgency? Or are you feeling unfulfilled and knowing there is a different life purpose for you, something coming from your inner truth? That truth is the calm place of intuition. Urgent, agitated and chaotic are sources of anxiety.

[3.] Glennon Doyle, "Episode 120: Jen Hatmaker's Back! Forgiveness and the Audacity to Rebuild." We Can Do Hard Things, August 8, 2022. Podcast, website, 1:11.
https://www.audacy.com/podcast/we-can-do-hard-things-d7b39/episodes/120-jen-hatmakers-back-forgiveness-the-audacity-to-rebuild-e9ebc.

There is also the simple act of asking:

- Does this belief ring true?
- Does it respect who I am?
- Does it restrict me from being who I am?
- Does it make me smaller?
- Does it encourage me?
- Does it motivate me?
- Does it challenge me to be my best Self?

An important part of this process is identifying what your beliefs are, even the ones you don't think are problematic. But also, are you acting in accordance with your beliefs? This can be tricky. Are you being a good, helpful person because that is Who You Are? Or are you striving to be a better, more helpful person than the next? Are you measuring your value based on *how* good and *how* helpful you are? Or are you looking to someone *else* to measure your value in this way? I'm not saying you shouldn't be a good, helpful person. Society emphasizes that for a reason. The point is, it shouldn't come before being Who You Are. When you truly love, you use your heart, soul, and mind. If you aren't loving yourself with the whole of your being, you aren't loving anyone else that way either because you aren't free to love.

One of the most important things I took away from counseling was that I was always free to leave. I may be staying today, but if I am not able to continue being me, I am free to leave tomorrow. That was a powerful realization. To understand that I am allowed to put my heart, soul, and mind first was a huge step toward shifting my mindset. It also gave me the freedom to determine what my boundaries were around leaving, meaning I could give myself space to build up my strength as much as I needed to first if the situation was still healthy enough for me to do so, but I could also leave quickly if it was not.

The Beliefs in Review

Looking back at the list of beliefs from ground zero, it was clear to me that I couldn't trust myself. There was no truth shining out of that belief ("Belief #1—I can trust myself"), though it was still a fundamental belief that I held. How does that work?! In all fairness, that's probably what turned me around and pointed me in the right direction. The truth was, I wasn't trusting myself, I wasn't listening to my own heart, soul, and mind, and I was in a bad spot. The result of that realization was I chose to *start* trusting myself, and that made all the difference. I started seeing the lies about me for what they were. I stopped allowing someone else to define my truth. I started building up from there. But, as I hope I have made clear, it took a long time for me to get to "how not to do it again." It's not magic.

"Belief #2—I am a good, helpful person" didn't seem to be a real problem at the beginning. I spent most of my time being a good, helpful person. That seemed the reasonable, socially expected thing to do. The fact that I was finding my value there, leaving other people to judge my value, was very late on my list of discoveries.

Eventually I realized there was some codependent behavior coming from that belief. I was trying to use my helpfulness (Ha! I mistyped that as helpful*mess* and nothing could be more true!) to control the lives of the people around me, to be all things to all people. But then, on top of the codependency, it dawned on me that I was also judging myself by my measure of goodness and helpfulness. The feedback I had received for years was that I was not good enough, that I was not worthy, so whatever I did never felt like enough. Letting go of the external judgment that I had internalized of who I was, allowed me to find my worth beyond helpfulness while still being a good, helpful person.

"Belief #3—I am smart, but I can't appear smarter than my partner" was a whole bundle of codependency and my internalization of sexism. I saw my partner's insecurity around my college education and chose to downplay my abilities. I lifted him up while pulling myself down. For the record, he is a smart person, and the insecurity was part of his larger problem of self-worth. Trying to "fix" that by making myself "less than" was just ridiculous and I make no excuses for it. It is what made the most sense to my mind at the time. That's about codependency. I should make him feel better about himself, even if he's being delusional, at my own expense. I can take it, I'm bigger than that. That's something I can control.

It was also about what I was being told and how I was being treated at the time. When you are treated as not being worthy of having your needs met, then you deny your needs and start to deny yourself. Your reality gets distorted to the point where your partner feels more important than you, your partner's needs become more important than yours, and their approval seems the only way for you to get back to approving of yourself.

I got caught in that trap. Here's how it works: I tried to build him up in ways that would be helpful for me. It seemed like it would be temporary; I give him the things that make me feel good about myself, he'll get better and we'll all be happy. He did not respond well to that because he doesn't work like me; he didn't want to lead. He hung out in Christian circles that kept reinforcing this idea that he needed to lead and he professed that as truth, but he wasn't comfortable leading. I felt worse about myself because I gave him the things that I needed to feel good about me. He felt pressured and his behavior toward me got worse. I was already down and his resentment confused and frightened me. This situation no longer felt like something I could control, and I couldn't figure out why. I kept waiting for him to have some kind of awakening, some realization that I have worth so that I could feel worthy. Please know, you are worthy. Don't wait around for anyone to tell you that. That fact does not depend on anyone else.

"Belief #4—I must guard my relationship, not only from outside, but from inside" was how families worked, in my experience. We hid our struggles from everybody, including ourselves. I was reading about different ways of being raised and the phrase "emotionally distant" jumped out above the rest. You put on the face; you do the things. Everything's fine, just fine. I chose the relationship I did partly because it was emotionally distant. It was easy, it didn't push me to examine myself; it was familiar.

I didn't want to downplay my existence, but I also didn't want to be a downer. I could list the bad facts of my life (not the bad feelings) in my Christmas letters and then put a positive spin in there (the dishwasher, refrigerator and septic all died this year, but hey, we have all new stuff!). I didn't want people to think poorly of my partner and I didn't want them to think poorly of my *choice* of partner. I think mostly that was because I didn't want to figure out how to explain it or rationalize it. Being transparent about the facts in my life made me *look* more emotionally present than I actually was. Facts are far different from emotions. I was available enough to have friends who felt they knew me.

"Belief #5—It is important to keep things steady and stable." That one is really just an extension of the last. Emotional distance rests on everything staying stable. Emotional flares require some kind of spark to set them off. The goal was always keeping the fires at bay. This kept the state of the relationship a secret because the state was all about drama and drama is not steady and stable. Steady and stable cut me off from my community because talking about it would create too much drama.

"Belief #6—Self-care is indulgent and not a priority" came later for me. As we went along, the relationship demanded more and more of my attention. As my self-esteem and security slipped away, it made self-care look extravagant. And as I blocked my emotions with busyness, self-care seemed like a waste of time. But also, subconsciously, I think I felt that self-care would give me time to feel, and I probably would not like what I felt.

"Belief #7—I have emotional muscle and I can muscle through anything" is related, though it came in earlier. I've always been very intuitive and could sense changes in body language and voice inflection that others would miss. Because of this, I felt the need to take care of people that were emotionally hurting and to not burden others with my own emotional pain. I think seeing it made it easier for me to control, and I understood that not everyone could see it the way I did. This is really the basis for my codependency; controlling all the things that make you feel bad so you don't have to feel bad. Whether I felt bad wasn't terribly important to me. Doing all of the things

Chapter Five

to control everyone else's feelings led me to turning off my own feelings. I couldn't handle them all at once, so I locked mine up where I didn't have to deal with them. As a human, let me tell you, that just doesn't work.

"Belief #8—I can rely on my smartness to figure it out" was how I lived my life from early on. I figured stuff out; it's what I did. Other people looked to me to figure stuff out. Logic and efficiency were my friends. The problem was, there were factors I didn't know or understand. People aren't always logical. I thought I could tell when people were lying, but when they believe their own lies it's really hard to tell what's a lie. People don't all think like me. To be honest, you just can't figure out people with smartness. People are wildly illogical. And intuition can be wrong because people don't always feel how you think they would. A much better use of your intuition would be to figure out your own motivations. Using it on other people might help in poker but, otherwise, use it sparingly.

"Belief #9—Partial is enough, I can (and should) fill in the rest." I think this one speaks to someone who is tired of being disappointed. You twist "I'm never going to find a perfect partner" into "I'll take what I can get." The reasoning is, if you can get some of your needs met, you'll make it work. But if this person isn't right for you, your relationship will suffer. Once it starts to decline, the partial things you had going for you start declining as well, until there isn't enough to sustain you. You don't need perfect, but you do need right. Right builds you up instead of tearing you down. The "should" part can come from your beliefs about marriage and/or divorce, your beliefs about how emotionally strong you are, pressure from your family and/or friends if your partner is someone they like or admire,

58

pressure from your church about male/female relationships, really anything that is telling you to stay and "fix" this relationship. "Should" is a clue that this is an external expectation coming from somewhere other than your truth. I never believed that I could fix him, but I did believe that I could fix the relationship. At this point, I'm not sure how I thought I could make that work, being only half of it, but you live and learn.

As you go through the grief in Chapter 4, you accept that you need to change in order to heal. Part of that acceptance is the mental work of actually choosing to change. Dig deep, find the core truth of your soul, and choose to change *for you*. Believe that you are worth changing for, you are worth the work. You are worth standing up for. You are worth protecting and nurturing. You can look at the choices you've made, reevaluate, and make new ones. You can reexamine your beliefs and tweak them or completely replace them. You have the power to be a newer, better version of you.

So... who do you want to be?

Chapter Six
Heal Yourself

I will admit I'm a bit of a geek when it comes to brain science, psychology, autoimmune conditions, body systems and how they interact, alternative medicine, nutrition, and all of those kinds of things. I am not a doctor, I took minimal science classes, and I have no professional training in anything science-related. I am not an expert, I just read a lot about things that fascinate me. I am also a mom with a daughter who has had an autoimmune condition for many years. You learn what you have to learn and you figure out where to find answers. Nothing in this book is meant to be medical advice because I am clearly not qualified to give it. I can only tell you what research says, what I think, what has worked for me, and why I think it worked or why I tried it.

My goal for this chapter is to cover some of the ways your body reacts to emotional distress and why it does what it does. All bodies have different histories, and emotional distress means different things to different people, so please don't think there is a specific answer for you in these pages. My hope is to give you ways to think about how your physical body is acting and reacting in relation to your emotional distress, and what that might mean to your day-to-day life.

I'm starting from the understanding that when you're in a bad relationship that leaves you with zero self-esteem, you spend a lot of time in fight-or-flight mode. That means your body detects a threat and switches to survival mode, making it more efficient at running away from or attacking the threat. Your body floods with hormones (like adrenaline and cortisol) that make this switch happen. Normally, you would expend this energy dealing with the threat, such as running away from a bear in the woods, and when the bear is gone your body would switch to relax-and-refuel mode and those hormones would fade. The 90 Second Rule (mentioned in Chapter 4) tells us that for most people, once a threat has passed, our body circuits will return us to normal within 90 seconds. When the threat becomes a way of life that doesn't resolve, it leaves your body confused about which hormones it should be producing when, and it leaves body systems not functioning properly. If this goes on for a long time, there are consequences for your body. Basically, I'm saying if your body is feeling pretty screwed up, I'm not surprised, and I'm hoping to help you with that.

There are a whole host of ways to understand your physical body responses. I often hear, "My body hates me." False! Your body is on your side. It is actually just doing what it was designed to do, reacting to threats and trying to keep you safe.

Let's go back to the fight-or-flight response. Health experts generally agree on how this response works on a physical level.

You feel threatened. Hormones like adrenaline and cortisol rush through your system. Those hormones cause your heart rate and blood pressure to increase, sending more oxygen and nutrients to the major muscles to create energy so you can run or fight. Blood flow is redirected from the extremities to the core. Pain response is diminished. Senses are heightened. There is a cost to that redirection of resources. As your body prioritizes the ability to run or fight, cortisol also causes it to deprioritize digestion, reproduction, and growth and repair.

What happens when that response doesn't turn off? Today's stress doesn't usually present itself as simply as being chased by a bear. There's not a clear start and end to the threat. This is where the confusion comes in about when to shut off the response. Our bodies are not meant to sustain long term stress. Deprioritizing your digestive system, or any system, for extended periods is probably not in your best interest.

According to the American Psychological Association, chronic stress can affect the following body systems:

- Musculoskeletal
- Respiratory
- Cardiovascular
- Endocrine
- Gastrointestinal
- Nervous
- Male reproductive
- Female reproductive.[4]

[4.] "Stress Effects on the Body," American Psychological Association, Nov. 1, 2018, updated March 8, 2023, accessed March 24, 2024 https://www.apa.org/topics/stress/body

As I said before, I'm not surprised your body feels screwed up. If you look at that list and think, "No wonder I don't feel good," I feel you. I'm not here to get into a long, technical explanation of the stuff that is going on in your body. Long-term stress is clearly a large barrier to good health and can manifest in many different systems, and as many kinds of symptoms.

I will stop to mention here that long-term stress can come from other areas of your life as well. It can come from many types of bad relationships, whether that be with a significant other, your own body, a family member, a neighbor, your church, your job, a friend or anyone else you are allowing to hold significant space in your life.

* * *

Again, there's an obvious question:

What do I do about it?!?

It may be obvious, but these issues come from storing up the effects of stress. Reducing the amount of stress in your life is probably the best place to start. If leaving the relationship is an option and would reduce your stress, then, if you can't justify it for any other reason, do it for your body. If leaving is not an option, or if it would not reduce your stress, then change your mindset. Just taking back control of your emotions is enough to reduce your stress. Remind yourself of the 90 Second Rule. If you get triggered, let the 90 seconds play out and remind yourself that you do not need to stay in that fearful state.

Take care of your body. This is of paramount importance because the better your physical body feels, the more you can work on the rest of it. Think about it—when your body is feeling terrible, how much harder is it to be positive and have hope?

But how, you ask? First, change your mind. Meaning if you don't consciously choose to change your lifestyle, and do it for you, to make yourself feel better, it won't mean much and won't last long. You are worth changing for. Hold onto that.

Once you decide to change, the question becomes, "where do I start?" What's your weakest link? At the time I chose to do the physical work, it was my back. My lower back kept going out and I kept going to the chiropractor to have him fix it. He gave me a few core exercises. I started doing them a few at a time. Start small! Ask a professional for advice on how to get started. Don't try to move mountains immediately, you will hurt yourself and set yourself back further than you were before. I increased the repetitions every few days, but I started at two or three. Listen to your body. If it hurts, cut back for a while. Trying to do just a few or modified repetitions is still helpful to keep you in the routine while you heal. If it still hurts, and not in a good way, you may want to get that checked out. Otherwise, keep at it. When it gets easy, increase again or add something new. Your physical issue may be your stomach, headaches, or something else. Whatever is recommended for you to treat it, start small, do a little bit each day, until you see improvement.

Eventually my back stopped bothering me. I increased strength in several areas which made everyday tasks easier. I didn't get as winded. My knees were stronger and more stable. My balance was better. I started feeling better. But also, I became more in touch with my body. When something wasn't right, it was easier for me to notice. I was able to find words to talk to my doctors about issues that were bothering me.

One of the issues I asked about led me to pelvic floor therapy. If you get the chance to do that, I highly recommend it. Because of my core work, I was able to get through pelvic floor therapy quite quickly, but it was very beneficial for me. I added exercises to my daily routine that used new muscle groups and loosened up some of those muscles that were in a constant state of tension. Again, it added stability by working muscles that supported other muscles. Tension weakens muscle, just like elastic that is always stretched wears out faster. Loosening the tension allows your muscles to heal. I learned a lot about how my body works and why the things I was doing were beneficial. I downloaded an app that reminded me how to do the exercises. It was such a positive experience and really helped my body.

I'm not saying you need to run marathons. Literally, whatever you can do is good. If you are so sick that you are stuck in bed, maybe all you can do is squeeze your fingers and toes. Start with that. Then do it more often. Maybe you can add some arm lifts. Then maybe move up to lifting a book. All of that is progress. Recognize your progress! Know that you are doing something helpful for yourself. It doesn't have to be huge; it's about moving forward. You may not be able to complete your routine every day; sometimes you have to back off and rest, and that's okay. It's about the overall trend being positive, not the daily ups and downs. Just don't let the downs become the lasting trend. It's the difference between skipping your exercises today because an old friend is in town and you want to hang out, versus skipping your exercises on a daily basis because you suddenly feel a need to talk to your neighbor. Make it a routine and learn to recognize and squash avoidance.

Maybe you're already running marathons. That's cool too. As long as you are doing it to feel good and not to punish your body, that's great. Are you listening to your body? Does running feel like freedom to you? That's when you know it's good for you. Or is it just another way to keep yourself busy and avoid feeling while feeding your need for adrenaline? That's something you might need to rethink.

Breathe. Try mindfulness, meditation or yoga. I will confess, this one is incredibly hard for me. Distraction is the way my stress-ninja brain deals with pretty much everything, and mindfulness is anti-distraction. Just remember, they use the word "practice" for a reason. It takes lots of practice. Mindfulness is a skill you need to learn. It doesn't magically happen. It is one of those things that being smart doesn't make easier. Try a few minutes at a time to start. It's not about the specifics, it's about controlling the breath, using the diaphragm (expanding your belly, not your chest), focusing, and learning to keep the distractions from derailing you when they come in.

You don't have to wait for the direction to breathe, count to a specific number, or "overbreathe" so you get dizzy. Calm your brain enough to listen to your body. Learning distraction management helps physically rewire your stress-ninja brain, and controlling breath changes the state of your autonomic nervous system, meaning it pulls you out of fight-or-flight mode. It's powerful stuff. If, like me, you find it just about impossible to focus, you might try a guided meditation or mindfulness exercise. Don't think, just do what you're told. Or you could try a mantra (repeating a word or phrase like "Om") so you have something specific to focus on. When your attention is drawn away from the practice, notice without judging and bring the focus back. There are apps that provide guidance if you feel you need some structure. Or join a yoga class if you need a separate space, a specific time commitment, or just a helpful person to lead you through it. Yoga adds a dimension of physical movement that helps with the release of stress.

You see a lot of information about Attention Deficit and Hyperactivity Disorder (ADHD) these days. If you relate to those symptoms and did not have them as a child, chances are it is just your stress-ninja brain trying to distract you from feeling the pain of losing your self-esteem, or whatever pain you may have, and from having adrenaline running through your system more often than not. Your body wasn't meant to do that. Do yourself a favor and learn to calm your brain and your nervous system through these practices. It will help you in many ways going forward.

Eat better. In all of the busyness of our controlling lives, it is hard to find the time to eat foods that are nutritious and healing. At this point, I think the whole scientific world agrees that ultra-processed foods are very bad for you. Unfortunately, ultra-processed usually means "easy to prepare." Sorry, but it's time to show up for your body. Use the time you gain being less controlling to commit a little extra time to finding, preparing, and consuming whole and less processed foods. If you have a problem with inflammation in your body, cut back on sugar, gluten and dairy, which are known to cause inflammation. There are lots of alternatives out there and lots of substitutions that are just a web search away. It takes effort and some trial and error, but it's a great step toward healing your body.

If you need help changing your diet and exercise habits, you may choose to consult with a health coach or nutritionist. They can help you set specific goals and give you tools to achieve them. If you have specific rituals or memories around food, changes here can be very hard. If food has been involved in your relationship or past in any negative way, that may have evolved into disordered eating. That is not my story, so all I can tell you is to seek help from a mental health professional or program. If you have been down that road in the past, check in with what that means to where you are now. You deserve to be healthy.

Once you start listening to your body, you will begin to notice what works and what doesn't. It will get easier when you start to see the benefits. I can tell you that dietary changes have allowed me to eliminate and reduce the maintenance medications that I was on. It really does help. Food can be very personal and can actually be its own bad relationship, so feel free to use this book on that level if that is what you need.

Sleep well. I am not a sleep expert, but, as a person who has experienced not sleeping for three full days, I can tell you sleep is really, really, really important. You can go from cranky to delirious pretty quickly. Because your body uses your sleep time to heal, if you're not sleeping, you are not healing. A quick web search will give you a list of ways to sleep better. If those don't work or don't even make sense to you, it's probably more about anxiety than sleeping.

For those of us trying to control our section of the universe, we can get pretty high levels of anxiety. Anxiety doesn't have to feel like worry, though it often does. Anxiety can feel like not being able to think clearly, not being able to make decisions, or not sleeping. When your first born is graduating from high school, your mom is showing signs of dementia, and your job is a struggle, along with your bad relationship, you may stop sleeping. Not that you're lying there thinking thoughts, something just shorts out and you have no thoughts, no relaxation, you're just awake. That's a real thing and they make meds for that. Go talk to your doctor. Getting sleep again gives you a far better perspective. Be sure your doctor checks your thyroid too, because problems there can affect sleep.

For a much more in-depth look at anxiety and how it works, check out Dr. Ellen Vora's book, *The Anatomy of Anxiety: Understanding and Overcoming the Body's Fear Response* (HarperCollins, 2022). It is spot on and so helpful in multiple ways.

Calm your nerves. The vagus nerve connects the brain, heart, and digestive system. Those fight-or-flight responses are communicated through the vagus nerve. Eighty percent of the signals in the vagus nerve are flowing from the body to the brain.[5] That means it's taking in information from the senses in your body and sending them to the brain to be processed. Twenty percent is flowing from the brain to the body. It takes all the information in, compares it to what it already knows, decides what to do, and sends the response signals back out. That's a lot of responsibility for one area, and keeping it on high alert all the time is probably not in your best interest. All of the above (exercise, breathe, eat, sleep) will help to calm the nervous system. If you want to add more to specifically target the vagus nerve, try gargling, laughing, singing or humming, the louder

---

[5.] Bessel Van Der Kolk, M.D., *The Body Keeps the Score: Brain, Mind and Body in the Healing of Trauma* (New York: Penguin Books, 2014) 83. 209.

the better. The vibration in your vocal cords stimulates the vagus nerve which helps you recover from the fight-or-flight response more quickly.[6]

Perhaps you've tried moving your body and getting some exercise and you are shocked at how little strength you have since the last time you noticed your body. Surprise! Cortisol decreases collagen production, and guess what your tendons and ligaments are mostly made of? That's right, collagen. Or maybe you've had gut issues for years. Cortisol affects enzyme activities, and fight-or-flight responses purposely cut back on digestion processes so you don't have to stop for a bathroom break while you're running through the forest. Your body is just doing what it was designed to do. A lot of people with chronic stress end up with chronic pain because these responses were not meant to be long term. There are reasons for the physical symptoms you have.

Point yourself in the right direction to get the care you need. You may not have a lot of physical complications yet and just need to restart an exercise routine or begin walking. You may have a bunch of complications and no idea where to start. Ask your doctor, chiropractor, naturopath, trainer, nutritionist, coach or whomever you trust to set you on the right path. As your body gains strength, you will begin to make the connection that you can trust your body. Building trust with your Self includes knowing your body, taking care of it, and giving it the respect it deserves for working to keep you safe.

[6.] Ashley Laderer, "5 Vagus Nerve Exercises to Help You Chill Out," Charlie Health (blog), January 5, 2024, accessed April 8, 2024. https://www.charliehealth.com/post/vagus-nerve-exercises.

This book concentrates on bad relationships. As I said at the beginning of this chapter, I am not a doctor. I am not really addressing trauma, not because I am minimizing the existence of trauma, but because I am not qualified to do so. I recognize that you may have experienced trauma as part of your bad relationship. That is real. If you have unresolved trauma from this relationship or from an earlier time, Dr. Bessel Van Der Kolk's book, *The Body Keeps the Score: Brain, Mind and Body in the Healing of Trauma,* discusses the ways that emotional and physical trauma are manifested in the physical health of the survivor. It is a fantastic book (it's not just me, it has over five years on the New York Times paperback nonfiction bestseller list[7] at the point of this writing) and I highly recommend it if you're really wanting to go deep into trauma's physical effects on the body. It can be hard to read because you can't really discuss the effects without mentioning the trauma. If you're having a hard time getting through it, skip to the second half of the book which talks about the various therapies and treatments that Dr. Van Der Kolk has found successful. I find a lot of hope there.

If you feel that trauma is affecting your physical and mental health, that section of the book may be helpful for understanding and choosing a therapy that feels right to you. I would encourage you to pursue treatment, with or without reading the book, because you are worth healing and you CAN heal.

[7] "Paperback Nonfiction," The New York Times, accessed November 26, 2023. https://www.nytimes.com/books/best-sellers/paperback-nonfiction/.

Chapter Seven
Love Yourself

For people in bad relationships, fighting or fleeing may not feel like an option. In that case, your body may get creative and go for the freeze or fawn options.[8] These options still have the same physical consequences because you are still feeling threatened, but there are additional elements at play.

Freeze is the "play dead" response to a threat when fighting or fleeing are no longer options. In the animal world, the lion has you in its mouth. This can literally shut down your body.[9] However, it can also manifest as your brain suppressing emotion (stop feeling) to deny the threat, especially if the threat is emotional as it often is in bad relationships. For example, if you are angry and telling me it's my fault, my freeze response could

---

[8] Carol A. Lambert, MSW, "Freeze and Fawn: Trauma Responses Undermine Self-Protection," Psychology Today, November 17, 2022, accessed November 26, 2023. https://www.psychologytoday.com/ca/blog/mind-games/202211/freeze-and-fawn-trauma-responses-undermine-self-protection.

[9] Bessel Van Der Kolk, M.D., *The Body Keeps the Score*, 86.

be to refuse to feel anything about that. Not feeling right or wrong or responsible, just plain not feeling. It's an attempt to trick the body into thinking the threat has passed.

The fawn response involves trying to appease the person who is the source of the threat in the hope of diffusing the situation and lessening the threat. "Hello, Ms. Lion, you're looking lovely today!" In the previous example, a fawn response might be for me to tell the person I'm sorry for making them angry (which, by the way, I did NOT do because they have their own feelings, I don't make them) and that it won't happen again, etc. It might also look like doing things you don't want to do because it's easier than fighting about it.

The problem with these responses is that you set aside your own self-preservation to avoid a threat. Let me make that clear. Your body is signaling "Danger! Run!" and you stay. You are able to bypass the urge to protect yourself and instead either stay rooted near the source of harm by denying your body response, or you engage with the danger, possibly even take responsibility for it. This is where those beliefs jump front and center, give you all the reasons you can't fight or flee, and try to come up with a way to exist in the presence of the threat. The danger isn't yours to control. You have control over your response to the danger. It seems simple, but getting those two ideas mixed up is at the core of how we got here.

When you sit with those faulty beliefs for a long time, it is a bit of a shock when someone looks you in the eye and says, "You can leave." I'm here to tell you, you can leave. You don't have to, but you can. This is why there is so much freedom in knowing that. You don't have to freeze or fawn anymore. You have the power to fight or leave. You have the freedom to listen to your body and to do what is right for you and your body.

The danger isn't yours to control. You have control over your response to the danger.

Bypassing the fight-or-flight response has led to your body being wildly confused because, not only are you dealing with long-term stress, you're now telling your body to ignore it. You are telling your body, "I'm choosing this." It does everything it can to signal that this is not sustainable. As we discussed in the last chapter, your body is trying desperately to save you. It's basically saying, "The invisible elephant in the room is squishing your organs! Can you not feel that?? Run! Fight! Do something! Anything!" When you make the choice to leave, stand up for yourself, and/or refuse to take responsibility for the bad choices the people you love are making and let them fall, you are rescuing your body and paving the way for emotional healing.

I make the assumption that you stopped feeling along the way because the chemical reactions in the fight-or-flight response cause you to block emotional response, as that is most efficient for getting away from a threat. Until you make the choice to do something, and stop those chemical reactions, you aren't physically able to do much work on emotional repair. This is also a good reason not to be too hard on yourself for not "figuring things out" much earlier. You didn't have the capacity.

I was not in a physically abusive situation, so when I made the decision that I was worth fighting for, I didn't have to leave to stop the fight-or-flight response. I flipped a switch in my head that showed me the things he had been saying were not true and that I did not deserve the way I was being treated. Seeing that and believing it are not the same thing, and it took time to internalize that, but I was able to stop the constant fight-or-flight response. I was slowly able to start processing what I was feeling. There was still a lot of fight-or-flight, but there was space in between. As I was able to process, I was able to create more space in between. Actually feeling took a long time and, even now, when I hit a bump in the road it's still very easy for me to stop feeling. But now I quickly notice and take measures to re-engage.

Looking back at the years before making that decision, I can see there were untreated bouts of depression and anxiety. We attended several rounds of marriage counseling that were not at all helpful. When you are lying to yourself and everyone around you, you aren't going to find lasting solutions. Even after making the decision to fight for myself, there were more rounds of counseling that did nothing. If you're not feeling heard or understood, please do yourself a favor and find a different therapist. If you're having a hard time getting past those freeze or fawn responses and things are constantly triggering those responses, you may just be stuck, or you may have Complex PTSD (post-traumatic stress disorder), which can be diagnosed in people with longer term trauma. You really should have professional help getting through any of these conditions, and I want to reinforce that help is not me. I'm just trying to help you put some words around what you may be feeling and to get yourself the help you need. In any case, I eventually found a therapist who heard me, and who referred me to another whose specialty was incredibly beneficial to my healing.

When you learn to reconnect with your body, you also learn to reconnect with your feelings. They are interrelated. Feeling the strength come back to weak muscles may ache, but it's sending the message, "you are getting stronger." It makes you feel good about what you are doing and helps motivate you to continue to exercise and move your body. As you start to feel stronger, you learn to trust your body. You lower your blood pressure, you take the stairs with confidence, you make better food choices, you reign in your acid reflux, or whatever is an improvement for you. That feeling of trust spills over into your mood, building your confidence in being able to handle what comes your way. You *feel* it.

In the same way, when you've shut off your feelings and you allow them to start coming back, they're going to ache. It works rather simultaneously, but starting with some physical confidence helps build and stretch that emotional confidence. You develop a good foundation for comparison. My body tells me I can feel better if I work through the ache; my feelings will probably be better if I work through the pain they hold. They are already better because my body feels better. There is hope.

Seeing a therapist was the weirdest experience for me. I hadn't felt anything for so long. I didn't have a safe space where I could express anything. She repeatedly told me, "You can leave." She gave me the space to think about that. But when I spoke to her alone it would usually end up with her asking me a question and me crying the rest of the time. That's what it feels like to be in a safe space, giving your body permission to let it out. She may not have thought she was doing much to help me, but that experience was so cleansing and helpful to my body. It helped to counteract the damage done by the long-term stress that was holding my body captive. Remaining in the relationship and having to consciously make the decision to not engage, and reinforce that I was worth it regularly, was its own kind of stress. I had been believing the opposite for a very long time. Making that shift is not easy, but it can be done.

Learn to trust yourself. Your feelings are in there. The most important thing you can do to begin recovery is find a piece of yourself you can trust. Find the part of yourself that wants to fight for you, that knows the truth of your worth, and work toward that. Know that you can heal. It feels like hope. Find a safe space where you can let your body release. Allow the sadness and the hope and the anger and the joy all to find their outlet.

Once you are able to feel, you can start creating. That may sound strange. Think about where your body is. If you've been running through a forest being chased by a bear, you're not writing sonnets. Once you've slammed the cabin door and locked it, you're exhausted. You're not painting pictures of your beautiful walk through the forest. If that bear is waiting every time you go outside, your every breath is focused on survival. Whatever you do to express yourself and make yourself feel understood by the universe is put on hold. Eventually that bear can go away and you will still have that reaction to going outside.

Allowing yourself to trust in your emotional safety is hard. A locked door doesn't remove emotional threats. Emotional threats are far less predictable than bears. Emotional threats can live in our minds long past the original threat. But they have the same result; they block us from connecting with our creative Self. The disconnection makes us feel more alone and less human. Once you can find some emotional safety you will be able to reconnect with what makes you feel human, whether that's going fishing or painting a masterpiece or enjoying the beauty of a walk in the woods.

If you look at your previous creative Self, it may give you clues as to where you need work or where things went off the rails. Though I never saw myself writing a book, I did enjoy writing. There was a time, long ago, when I wrote song lyrics. I also wrote in a journal. Looking back now, you would think two different people wrote them. The journal said all of the things I was trying to convince myself were true and it felt completely false. Of course, at the time, it felt reasonable... but it didn't flow. The song lyrics, on the other hand, sliced me open and just laid it all out there. There was my truth, and it would not be contained. It's when I started stifling my truth that things went awry. I stopped writing altogether. Your situation may not be that clear cut, but you may see something like, "there was this thing I liked to do, and then I stopped doing it." Or maybe you just stopped doing it well. You lost that connection to your truth. That thing, that connection, is so important. It connects you not only to yourself, but to the universe. You feel more alive, loved, more human and less alone.

Maybe you don't know what your thing is. To be honest, I would have guessed painting to be my thing. The more I write, the more it becomes clear that this is how I connect and express my truth creatively. It will come to you. Do what makes you feel good and true and don't worry about it. It can be new things. It can be multiple things. Listening to a whippoorwill on a quiet summer night makes me feel connected. Talking with my cousins makes me feel connected to our childhood and staying at grandma's house. The point is to get to a place where you are emotionally available to feel that connection with anything.

I started writing as soon as I was able to interrupt the fight-or-flight response. I wasn't really feeling yet, but I was processing, and writing allowed me to process. None of it was terribly coherent, but it set me on the path of creating the me I wanted to become. It helped me sort out what the feelings might be if I allowed them and prepared me to deal with them. It helped me find words to communicate what I needed. It gave me a direction to get to me. It allowed me to see my value and gave me something to fight for. It helped me to see my value is not in what I do, but in my connection with all things. It's not in the end result, being a song or a book, it's about the process of putting myself into it and finding myself in it. If going fishing is what does that for you, do it. Do the thing.

Chapter Eight
Love Others

People need people.

I will stand by this until my dying breath. I am wildly introverted and enjoyed the relative quiet of COVID quarantine, but I'm still here to tell you that people need people. Scientific studies tell us young children who don't get enough human engagement and touch have a variety of issues, including higher levels of cortisol (there's that word again) years later.[10] Prisoners who are placed in solitary confinement face a laundry list of negative effects on all aspects of their health, to the point where the United Nations considers more than 15 days of solitary confinement as torture.[11]

---

[10] Katherine Harmon, "How Important Is Physical Contact with Your Infant?," Scientific American, May 6, 2010, accessed November 26, 2023.
https://www.scientificamerican.com/article/infant-touch/.
[11] Tiana Herring, "The Research is Clear: Solitary Confinement Causes Long-Lasting Harm," Prison Policy Initiative, December 8, 2020, accessed November 26, 2023.
https://www.prisonpolicy.org/blog/2020/12/08/solitary_symposium/.

I know. People stress you out. And now I'm telling you *no* people stresses you out. Why is that a thing? Why do I need people? What is the purpose?

I'm no mountaintop guru, so I'm going with the Beatles on this one. My guess is it's all about love. Just as babies don't thrive without love, we too fail to thrive without love. As I mentioned earlier, we can't fully love without loving ourselves first. But how do we learn to love ourselves? We receive love from others. When we lose our love of Self (the self-esteem I've been talking about throughout this book), love from others helps show us the way back.

We lost that self-esteem because we felt unlovable and unworthy of love. No wonder we're feeling tortured and not thriving! We are walling ourselves off from people and putting ourselves in a place of solitary confinement. Please hear me loud and clear: You are lovable and amazingly worthy of love. There is nothing you did or could do that would make you unworthy of love. Bad choices happen, accidents happen, bad things happen, but that is all they are, no more, no less. They don't define your value or make you less lovable. They do make you an ordinary human. There is nothing you could or should have done to control what someone else thought, said, or felt about you. That someone has the choice to believe what they want. They are human and allowed to make bad choices. They do not define you. You define you.

Let's pause for a moment and go back to Chapter 3 on how to tank a relationship. Specifically, look at point #4. "You are betraying yourself, feeling shame and responding poorly." When I say betraying yourself, I mean you are allowing the other person to define you. That definition doesn't mesh with who you know you are and the result is shame. It's not who you are, it's not who you want to be, and it's not who you want the people you love to see. That last part of shame is where loneliness comes in. Again, you are walling yourself off from the people who love you and who could help show you the way back to loving yourself.

In my world, the result of the shame of the relationship is that I didn't discuss it with my network. I would only share what would make my partner look good or at least neutral. I didn't want him to be hated because then I would be pressured to make a decision. But also, I didn't want to risk sullying their view of me (losing their respect) by allowing them to think of me as the one who would accept that kind of behavior. I generally stayed away from my network because, in my opinion, they would get tired of hearing about it if I wasn't going to do anything about it, and I didn't want to do that or talk about it. The people I did interact with got the surface stuff; we didn't go deep.

You don't deserve to be tortured. Let yourself out of solitary confinement. I knew I needed to do that, but I had no idea how. Again, I am an introvert; this is not my skill set. I do watch other people who have the skill I want. Think about the relationships you find most helpful. What do they look like? What kind of interactions feel the most connecting?

This is probably around the time where I realized I didn't want to do this again, and I was really concerned about making good choices. Here are some ideas I came up with for building a network:

1. Start small—Having a party for a bunch of people may be fun, but it's not likely to build a connection. Try getting together with one or two people at a time.

2. Pre-relationship friends—Reach out to an old friend or two that you feel comfortable with. Reconnect, ask questions, be honest about where you are.

3. Start fresh—Maybe you burned your bridges, maybe you feel you need a different crowd, maybe you've never felt very supported. When you are doing your thing, the thing that you create when you are feeling, pay attention to the people around you. If your thing is more solitary, like writing, maybe take a class, or offer to share it or teach it. Find people with similar interests or similar locations and be open to talking to them. Be open to seeing the people around you. If you're not sure what your thing is, try something new. When something looks interesting, take action! Take the steps to try it or learn about it or join a community to talk about it.

4. Be clear—You need a friend, not a romance at this point in time. You have some building to do first. If they don't respect that, move on. Not that you can't find romance, but be sure you're in a place where you feel whole and you're not looking for someone to fill a void.

5. Make it an actual network—Build a network of five friends that you can talk to. Understand that people have lives and they can't always drop everything to come to your aid. Give yourself some options and give them the freedom to say no if they need to.

6. Be a good friend—Just as you will need support, know that your friends aren't perfect and they will also need

support. Don't only show up when you need something. Here's where you find limiting your network is useful because supporting too many may leave you feeling overwhelmed.

7. Build healthy relationships—Use your words. Tell your people how best to support you and ask how you can support them (you don't have to fix me; I just need x).

8. Develop healthy boundaries—This will take some work. A simple one is: know your truth and stand up for it and yourself. Always know you can leave. A fantastic resource to get specifics on this is *The Book of Boundaries* by Melissa Urban. It provides actual words to use for anything from special diets to mothers-in-law and covers what makes a boundary healthy and why you need them.

What does love and support look like? This whole process of "how not to do it again" can be exhausting. Friends are there to remind you that you are worth the effort and you are lovable. When you get too far in your head, they can gently lead you back out. They have a different perspective as someone looking at the relationship from outside. They can point out faulty logic. And they can make you laugh and forget about it for a while.

I once heard a story about a little boy who couldn't get his toy unstuck. His father asked, "Are you using all the strength available to you?" The boy said yes, but he hadn't asked his dad to help him. Sometimes you need to ask yourself, "Am I using all the strength available to me?" It may be as simple as asking for help from a friend.

If you are having problems creating a network and need help figuring out how to make friends, think about why you want friends in the first place. Do you have trouble receiving love and support? Do you believe you deserve that? What gets in your way when trying to build new or closer connections? Don't be afraid to get some mental health counseling around these questions. That is just another, hopefully less threatening, way of connecting with another human. Your counselor may not "love you" in the way that you were thinking, but if they love what they do, and you're a part of that, then there's still love to be had there. It's also a good way to practice connecting with humans. If you're feeling like a feral cat around people, counseling is a very low-key way to re-socialize yourself. Role-playing and other mental health tools can go a long way toward making you feel comfortable meeting and talking to people.

"Okay, sure," you say. "I need people. But I need to do this for myself."

Absolutely. You must do this FOR yourself. You must not do this BY yourself. You're running from the bear FOR yourself. (Good job, you chose to survive.) You're choosing to recognize your value and worth FOR yourself. (Good job, you chose to trust your truth.) In the same way, you are choosing to have friends FOR yourself. It is a necessary component of becoming the healthy, happy human you want to be. It is choosing an existence that doesn't feel like torture. If you are being something that doesn't make you feel lovable or valued FOR your friends, those are not the friends you want. If you are being anything but honest FOR the people you love, you are going right back where you came from. Choose your friends wisely and always know, "You can leave."

That brings us back to where you were, letting other people define you. And where you want to be; letting you define you.

How do you want to define yourself?

You have to make the choice to believe positive things about you. You are lovable. You are worthy of love. You are valuable. You deserve love. If that sounds foreign to you, that's where the majority of your work will be. Once you believe those positive ideas about yourself, you can do the mental, physical and emotional work FOR you. Once you believe those truths, you will attract friends. Once you believe in your positive identity, you will open up spiritual pathways that connect You to greater things.

When you consciously define yourself in this way and believe it to your core, doing the work to realign your life with this definition becomes natural *because* you are doing it FOR you. You are loving yourself because you are worthy of love. Having good friends is natural because you are *being* a good friend, able to give and receive love freely.

The problem with being social is you can only control you. **You can only control you.** No asterisk, no but, period, that is all. People are notoriously messy. We all have our baggage and occasionally the airport finds it and delivers it when we're least expecting it. Other people get to be a mess sometimes. That's okay. It's not your job to fix it. It's not your job to predict it. It's not your job to judge it. It's not your job to agree or disagree with it. Your job is to love and support them and remind them of their worth.

You get to be a mess sometimes. You may have triggers that send you back to that place of no self-esteem and insecurity. It happens. Your friends are not there to fix it, predict it, judge it, agree with it or disagree with it. Their job is to love and support you and remind you of your worth. Your job is to recognize as quickly as possible that what you are feeling is coming from an old belief. Use the tools you've learned to reaffirm your worth. Investigate what sent you to this place, and consider whether there is something you have yet to resolve related to it. If you had an unexpected response to a friend's actions, it's okay to tell them, "I'm sorry. I have been conditioned to react this way when *x* happens. I realize that's not about you and does not reflect the way you treat me. I'm still working on it." Maybe the next time you won't be taken back to that place, or you will recover faster. Allow yourself to not be perfect.

You may be fearful of people. Bad or abusive relationships often isolate by design, in order to hide the badness or abuse and/or to lessen the opportunity to leave. If you have been conditioned to avoid contact with people through fear, "putting yourself out there" is going to be hard. Take it slow, start small, begin with people you know or events that involve one of your creative things. In other words, choose to expose yourself in a way that connects with you in some way. Work through the issues as they come up. Hold onto your connection for stability. Leave when you start feeling overwhelmed. Give yourself credit for effort. Again, try to note the specific triggers so you can process through them and learn from them. Fear is the opposite of love so, if you can, try to send love from yourself into the situation to push back the fear. Look for beauty and things that touch your heart so you have a well of love to pull from. You can't fear and love at the same time.

People will disappoint you. I know we already covered this, but people make bad choices. They just do. You get to control how you respond to their bad choices. If those choices affect your safety, you can choose to survive. If those choices affect your self-esteem, you can choose to trust your truth and/or walk away. If you have differing opinions of whether it was a bad choice, you get to choose your own opinion and respond accordingly. Knowing how this works is how you learn to build boundaries.

Boundaries are how you protect yourself from other people's choices. The core to setting boundaries is having that self-esteem and security, loving yourself enough to stand up for you, and knowing you are worth standing up for. When you have that, you can set effective boundaries. Boundaries are not telling other people what they can do. Setting a boundary involves identifying the behavior that is affecting you, communicating a realistic consequence of the behavior, and following up with that consequence if the behavior doesn't change. For example, the neighbor's kid likes to fish and comes into your cabin wearing muddy boots. You tell her she needs to leave her muddy boots outside or she is no longer allowed in your cabin. She continues to wear the muddy boots; you lock the door.

This is a very simplified example. Suppose you are lonely and the child is the only one that comes to visit you. The consequence in this instance would be punishing yourself over muddy floors. Is it worth it? It has to be something you are willing to do. Boundaries can be flexible. You're probably not going to lock the door if she's being chased by a bear. That seems a bit unethical. It also has to be something you can control. You can't tell the child she is expected to clean up the mud. You can ask her to do that, but it is not a consequence. It is completely under her control whether she cleans up the mud or not. The answer to building good boundaries (and in leaving codependency behind) lies in knowing what you can control and what you can't. The consequence has to be what *you* will do when the behavior happens.

The answer to building good boundaries (and in leaving codependency behind) lies in knowing what you can control and what you can't.

Again, please check out *The Book of Boundaries* by Melissa Urban. There are a ton of real-life relationship examples with sample words to use in many situations. She uses a tiered green-yellow-red approach where the consequences get tougher if the behavior continues. It is very helpful in situations that have a tendency to escalate. She points out that, often, all it takes is voicing what you want and the "green" boundary is enough. The bad relationship can leave us thinking that speaking up is pointless, so we neglect to even try boundaries when, really, they are effective most of the time. Healthy boundaries are key to letting people in without allowing them to step on your self-esteem.

I know this all sounds much simpler than it actually is. The last thing you want to do is make yourself vulnerable to other people, considering how it ended up the last time. I get that. But consider that the person you've been hiding from most is yourself. Getting vulnerable with yourself, allowing yourself to be open to exploring and healing your wounds, and getting in touch with your truth will open up ways for you to enter healthier relationships and be better equipped to handle the ones you are already in. It may actually make you miss people you've lost touch with, people that were good for you. Wanting people in your life is a natural part of healing. Having support around you is helpful to healing. People need people.

Chapter Nine
Connect to a Larger Framework

The problem with zero self-esteem is that your sense of Self gets distorted. You not only lose the love for yourself from inside, you lose your connection with the larger universe that helps you find love from the outside. That connection makes you feel worthy of love. Without that connection, all of the work you're doing to pull yourself up feels meaningless and shallow. Your worth isn't found in what you do or say, or what you control. Your worth is found in being part of a larger picture, connected to all things and being part of the creative processes going on around you all of the time.

In my mind, the larger framework I am referring to is the way all lives are connected. As parts of this larger framework, we each have the power to create. If we are feeling unworthy and unloved, our negative energy will be used to create negative experiences. We may stop creating because we feel powerless. We perpetuate the negative. If we can learn to feel loved and accepted in our truth, and connected to a greater truth, we attract positive energy. Our power will be used to create things or experiences that are based in our truth—the things we were made to create. The negative or positive nature of our spirit (that part of us that exists as energy) tends to create experiences that match that status. If you want positive things to happen in your life, focus on having positive energy from which to create them. Your spirit takes what is within you and connects it to the world around you. If your thoughts all center on you, you won't have much reach into the universe, and you will feel disconnected.

When I say "find love from the outside," I'm not talking about romantic love. I'm talking about that feeling of love that surrounds you when everything is right with the world. I know it's hard to get in touch with that, but think about what that means to you. To me that looks like being healthy and strong, able to dance and sing, surrounded by the beauty of nature, not trying to control anyone else, living in the truth about me, and able to share that truth with others through my writing. It's the feeling that I can breathe. You may feel at one with the universe walking down a busy street, feeling the ebb and flow of the crowd move you. Or maybe it's standing in front of an audience, or running through a field. You don't have to fit any specific mold. We all have a place in the universe and, while we have lots of things in common, we all have different things that make us feel whole.

Maybe you can't remember what love or being at one with the universe feels like, so you don't know what that looks like for you. There's nothing wrong with you; it's just a disconnection. Be gentle with yourself. What makes you feel like you can breathe? What causes your body to relax? You might see tips from the other chapters come back to you here because they're all trying to get you in touch with You. Plugging in to Who You Are helps you connect with the universe because the universe doesn't deal in lies. Getting to your truth shows you how you fit into the greater framework of the universe and connects you to it. Your truth is your worth, and the universe loves you exactly for who you are because that's who you were made to be.

Maybe that all feels a little woo-woo for you.

You could look at it as connecting to your future Self. Who do you visualize your future Self to be? To me, that is what I described above. There's nothing woo-woo about wanting my future Self to be healthy and be at peace with who I am and what I'm doing. It may feel woo-woo when I talk about connecting with the universe. When I am feeling that peace, that's what it feels like to me. I am no longer in solitary confinement. Being alone does not feel lonely. I feel connected. I'm saying "connected to the universe" because I'm not going to dictate who or what you connect with. You could call it connecting with a deity or a savior or a prophet, or getting closer to reaching nirvana or enlightenment. You are welcome to use whatever makes sense for your connection in place of "the universe." Just know that it is bigger and longer-lasting than any one person, community, or idea. It really does connect you to all things.

Action

When I talk about connecting to your future Self, I don't mean you should focus on the future. It's about actually *being* that future Self now. It's connecting who you are now to that vision of the future by believing it and living it now. It's about asking yourself, "Is this beneficial to becoming my future Self? Would my future Self do this?" However, if you focus on the "future" part, you will never get there; it will always be ahead of you. You connect to that future Self by acting on it now, bringing it into being. It is an act of creation, which is how it becomes a spiritual connection.

When your truth shows you Who You Are, you need to pay attention. Once you see it, you have choices to make. Your truth connects you to your future Self, but, as you are well aware, you don't always stay true to your truth. The universe will put opportunities for your true Self in your path. Pay attention and take action when they arise. Action will keep you on the right path with the least amount of detours. If you don't act, opportunities to live more fully will pass by.

Fear is the biggest roadblock between you and where you want to be. Fear will cause missed opportunities and can bring your faulty beliefs back from the past. Fear and love can't coexist, so learn to recognize your hesitation and doubt as fear. Jump on that right away. Where is it coming from? Why? What looks familiar here? What thoughts and feelings are coming up? If I expect love here instead, what would that look like?

Some people just know their truth and will go through whatever needs to happen to be their true Self, seeking out opportunities and taking action wherever possible. Others are not really sure what that looks like. What does my future Self want? Where do I want to be? I'm good at a lot of things, but nothing really seems like "it." That is completely normal—please don't feel like there's something wrong with you. Keep going in the direction of what feels true. The more you love and prioritize yourself, do the things that make you feel creative and talk to people about them, the closer you will get to finding your thing. Saying "I can't" blocks the universe from showing you Who You Are. Saying "I have to" or "I should" makes it about what someone else expects of you. Do what you *want* to do. Explore the things you are drawn to. It's a process. Be positive. Be intentional. Be patient and, again, be open to act when opportunities arise.

If I expect love here instead, what would that look like?

Society may or may not be accepting of the You that is your truth. The important thing is that you are accepting of yourself. Know that there are others out there like you. You are not alone. You are not unlovable. You are worthy of love. When you accept your truth, the universe welcomes you to Who You Are with love. That feels like home. That's bigger than you; you will find a community there.

Gratitude

Being part of that bigger picture, feeling connected, and visualizing your future Self as whole and worthy can be really hard to grasp. Getting familiar with how the universe leads you to the next thing and trusting that it will provide those opportunities truly is an act of faith. Yes, you worked hard to get here. But once you start paying attention to the way the universe guides your path, you will see that you weren't the only one blazing your trail. Feeling gratitude is a way to acknowledge that you have felt supported and loved by all that you are connected with. It helps to bring all of the woo-woo feelings that you're not quite sure about into a solid, grounded practice of just saying "thank you."

"Thank you for that lunch with a friend, who pointed me to that book, which got me interested in that author, which sent me on an exploration of that topic that got me to this latest realization about where my beliefs came from." This kind of stuff doesn't just happen. For example, my dad died suddenly, at a relatively young age, while on vacation. Over the lunch hour on the day he passed, I got sidetracked on some topic and spent waaay too much time digging through several websites on grief. That night, he had a heart attack and died before reaching the hospital. The ER doctor called to inform me and have me talk to my mom. "Thank you for preparing me."

It takes some practice to tune in to and recognize these cues from the universe as important to your continued development and to act on them. You have to suppress the urge to talk yourself out of them with words like "coincidence" and "waste of time." If you tune in, you will be able to tell which things the universe is pointing toward. They will just feel important. You will be drawn to them. Explaining that is weird. I'm not saying you have to explain it. I'm saying, when it happens, it's appropriate to act and to be grateful. Being grateful is not weird. It is between you and your connection, and gives recognition of that loving relationship.

You don't have to be perfect to make this connection. You don't have to wait until you're fully healed. You don't even have to know what your beliefs are. You can be starting at square one. You just have to see a glimmer of truth or something that feels positive and important and aim for that. Maybe that's what brought you to this book. Spiritual connection is a creative process. Leaning into it will help you to create the Self you want to be.

Part III: Trust Yourself Enough to Move On

Chapter Ten
Know Your Truth

As I look back at where I've been, I can see where my old beliefs threw me off track. I can see how I made unhealthy choices and why they were unhealthy. I did the work and my beliefs have changed to reflect the work I have done. This is not to say that the old beliefs don't pop up from time to time, but when they do I have the tools to recognize them, confront them, and reject them as false. Sometimes I recognize them quickly, and other times it takes a while, but the key is to recognize them. I may also find new beliefs that are/were harmful to me and my relationships. I am open to exploring ideas that don't feel true to decide whether they need work. Life goes on with its ups and downs, but I have skills and I can learn new ones if I need to.

When you examine your beliefs, there are questions you can ask that get to the core of who you are:

- Where have I been lying to myself?
- Where have I been finding my value?
- What have I been hiding?

- What have I been avoiding because it feels uncomfortable?
- Do I have fears that are unreasonable?
- What are my strengths?
- Where am I getting stuck?
- What makes me feel whole?
- Does my body feel trustworthy?
- Is there anything blocking my emotions?
- What gives me hope?
- When do I feel relaxed?

Once I figured out what I believed and how those beliefs were affecting my life, I was able to visualize "how not to do it again." Reframing my beliefs into a list that felt right and true was what I needed to hold myself to a different standard, one that treated me as a smart, honest, vulnerable person who is able to be seen as she is, not as someone else wants her to be. Because I am valued for who I am, I am able to take care of myself, set boundaries and stand up for me. Here's how my beliefs look now:

The Rewritten Beliefs

1. I can trust myself when I am being honest with myself. (Ch 5)
2. I am a good, helpful person, but that is not where I find my value. (Ch 5)
3. I am smart and I don't have to hide it. (Ch 2 & 5)

4. I must guard my own boundaries to maintain my mental health and stay true to me. (Ch 8)
5. Keeping things steady and stable doesn't allow me to grow. Fear blocks my growth. Embracing the uncomfortable for a time helps me become better. (Ch 5 & 9)
6. Self-care is a high priority. If I don't take care of Me, I can't be good at caring for anyone else. (Ch 4 & 6)
7. I have emotional muscle, and I can use it to pull out of negative thoughts. I don't need to deny my emotions or wallow in them, just recognize them, feel them, and continue to move all the way through them. (Ch 4 & 5)
8. I can rely on my smartness and problem-solving ability, but life isn't always logical. Sometimes I'm starting from a faulty belief. I don't have to be perfect. It's okay to ask for help when I don't understand or get stuck. (Ch 2, 5 & 7)
9. I am a whole person with my own thoughts, emotions, talents, hopes, dreams and goals. If I want to be in a relationship, my significant other should see me as a whole person and should be a whole person themselves. (Ch 12)

These beliefs feel true to me. They allow me to be who I am, which is smart but still human. They remind me that I have the capacity to grow and manage my own thoughts. They leave space for me to take care of myself and set limits, but also to be vulnerable while still being myself with others. They don't feel limiting to me. I feel like I can be who I was created to be within these beliefs. How are your beliefs limiting you? What if you chose new beliefs that removed those limits? What could you do?

When I open myself to all of my thoughts, body responses, and emotions, and do the work to align them with who I am, I can start to trust myself again because the truth is that I wasn't trusting myself. I chose to place my faith in what other people told me rather than what I knew to be true. Building that trust is the first place to begin to remove your limits. Practice listening to Who You Are to build that trust. Give it your attention and place confidence in what you hear. That confidence is the basis for trusting yourself enough to move forward.

How are your beliefs limiting you? What if you chose new beliefs that removed those limits?

Give yourself permission to like you and root for you. Choosing to love yourself derails shame. When you stop judging yourself, accept yourself, and choose to be on your own side, you move away from shame and fear. Most of us have some beliefs that tell us it is not acceptable to be who we really are. I'm here to tell you that Who You Really Are is the only acceptable way to be. Anything else is a lie. Tying yourself in knots to prove that you are not You pulls you farther from Who You Are and closer to being miserable, whether you're in a bad relationship or not. Going through the steps to figure out Who You Are, doing the work to realign with that and rewriting your beliefs to reflect what is true for you can be terrifying. It is a LOT. But when you look at your life and you see freedom and truth flowing in and around you, then it becomes easier to see and become Who You Really Are.

If Who You Really Are causes you to bring harm (physical, financial or otherwise) to other people or yourself, it's very likely that the actual Who You Really Are is still a few layers deeper than that. If you decide Who You Really Are is a serial killer or pedophile, please seek professional help immediately. Sometimes we need to keep fluffing those blankets to find that bottom layer.

Suppose you have a belief that your family, your religion, your community, or some other person or group that you trust has instilled in you. What happens when Who You Really Are doesn't agree with that? Have you ever prayed or wished to be less *(bold, audacious, quiet, flamboyant, You, etc.)* than you are? If that word/adjective is your truth, think about why you would pray or wish that. What belief do you have that would make you ask to be less than Who You Are? I think the trusted relationship becomes a bad relationship in this instance. You either bury Who You Really Are and end up doing all the things this book is trying to help you work out of, or you choose to be yourself and reevaluate that trusted relationship.

As I've said many times in this book, that doesn't mean you have to leave the relationship. It does mean you have to step back and decide how much space you are going to allow it to hold in your life, and how you are going to define your truth. You may want to do some research to see what other families/religions/communities, etc. believe about the topic. It may be a matter of education or a tradition you can live without. It may be a deal breaker that finds you rejected from that space. That happens. That presents another choice. Do you bury your Self, or do you go find another family/religion/community that better aligns with Who You Are? Goodbye is not easy. Finding your people is not easy. Being buried alive is not easy. I highly recommend you keep choosing truth, but I get that not everybody has options. At least recognize that it's a conscious choice, and you can always choose to leave later.

Choose loving yourself over making other people comfortable. The act of choosing to be All of You with the people around you on a more personal level can be intimidating to both you and them. Not that you should try to be intimidating. Part of being All of You is also being vulnerable and allowing your weaknesses to show as well as your strengths. But if you are intimidating even with that balance, then that perception is the choice of the other person and you aren't responsible for that. Continue to be Who You Are and don't feel pressured to be less than that. Loving yourself includes letting Who You Are be your default mode of existence. Again, there may need to be a shift in how much space you allow certain people to hold in your life.

It's still okay to be a good, helpful person. Your truth can live inside that. As a spiritual being connected to the universe, being good and helpful comes naturally. You don't have to be a good, helpful person every minute of every day, or for everyone you meet. Your value is not tied to being good and helpful. If someone is taking advantage of your helpfulness or if it doesn't feel right, you can choose not to be helpful or to stop being helpful in that moment. You can place boundaries on your time and resources and still remain a good and helpful person. As they say, put on your own oxygen mask first. You have to keep yourself healthy or you will be no help to anyone else.

Give yourself permission to want something. When you disconnect from and deny yourself, you tend not to give yourself the attention you need. Things you want get pushed to the bottom of the list or off the list altogether. Get back on the list. What will help you get to where you want to be? What will feed your future Self? As you start to see your truth, certain ideas will start coming up. Stay open to them. Don't think "I can't" or "I won't" when these ideas present themselves. It's okay to see something new and different. Try looking at it from the perspective of "What if?" Is it really not something you can do? Or are you putting artificial barriers in your own way? Do the research, think of it positively, use encouraging words to describe it. All of these actions will move you toward creating the outcome you want. If this is something you can picture for yourself, visualizing and the positive energy you put into it can bring it closer to reality.

I know that throughout my bad relationship, I was overestimating my strength and underestimating my value. I see now that my strength has limits and using it to stop my own negative thoughts is far more helpful than trying to keep everyone in my circle from feeling anything negative. I can also use my strength to allow myself to be vulnerable when in the past I would wall myself off. These acts of strength will build me up and bring me more strength rather than less. Knowing my value, that I am not "too much" or "not enough," also builds me up and allows me to stand up for myself and set healthy boundaries. It gives me clarity about what I can control and what is out of my control. Taking care of myself in this way reinforces my value. Building myself up and protecting Who I Am brings me closer to my truth.

Some people get really hung up on needing to forgive the person/people who hurt you. If you're stuck on that idea, then definitely work through that. I'm all about letting that idea go. I don't think it's about them so, in my opinion, it's only going to help as much as getting you to stop obsessing about them helps. That could be quite a lot, and I am in favor of working through that.

But also, I am in favor of you forgiving yourself. If somewhere deep inside you is the creator of old beliefs, rocking back and forth and thinking you did something wrong, "you brought this all on yourself," or "you made this happen," just stop. So what if you did? You are allowed to make mistakes. You are not perfect. You are human. That's what makes you beautiful. Why does there need to be someone to blame? Of what use is that? Where is that coming from?

You did the best you could in the circumstances you found yourself in. Your experiences kept building on each other. Some you chose, some you didn't. Just stop. You don't need to take responsibility for the actions of others; I think we've covered that at length. Of the parts that are left, so what? What if you are suffering the consequences of your own decisions? I think we've also covered that fight-or-flight mode doesn't really have access to reasonable thought. How much of what you did was done in fear? What experiences does that leave to your reasonable decision-making? Forgive yourself for making decisions that ended up hurting you. Recognize your own beauty. Commit to learning from your mistakes and taking care of yourself. There is no reason to worry about where to put the blame.

Maybe your truth involves past trauma and mental health issues. This book is not likely to fix that. Please know that if the tips don't work for you, it's not because "you're doing it wrong." It means they don't work for your brain. For example, if you have bipolar disorder, the 90 Second Rule is not likely to pull you out of a manic episode. If you have PTSD and you feel triggered, you may not feel safe enough to take care of yourself at that moment. Remember that you are not always in that hypervigilant state. You can still use this book to work through thoughts and feelings around the bad relationship when you are able. You will have some extra challenges, but be patient with yourself. There is no time limit. You can still heal. You can still find your truth.

Chapter Eleven

Your Old Life Will Still Be There; Use Your Skills

I have purposely left your partner out of most of this book because it's not about them. It's about you and your healing process, and the things you can control. As much as you may have tried in the past, I'm hoping by now you realize that you cannot control your partner.

If you have left, don't be surprised if your partner shows up again, even if they are the one who initiated the end. In their world, it's likely all your fault and yet they will want your support. You will get all kinds of mixed messages. We have established that your partner is more comfortable following than leading. They are used to having you take care of them. That is part of codependency. They depended on you to fix their problems, and now they are likely a hot mess. This is normal and you need to know it is not your responsibility. Know that you deserve better and you do not need to support them. They are responsible for their own choices and actions. You are responsible for you.

Chances are this was a stressful, fearful relationship. You going back to save the day will only put you in the position of taking on the consequences of their actions. It is time to break the codependency cycle and let them take on their own consequences. You do not need to be friends and you do not need to be polite, but you can if you want to. You DO need to create boundaries and be clear about them.

If you are still in the relationship, boundaries are even more important. But also really important is knowing this: even if you have agreed to stay, you ALWAYS have the option to leave. You may have just agreed to stay yesterday, doesn't matter. If and when you feel it is unsustainable and you have to go, you have the option to go, and leaving is a reasonable thing to do. If you feel you are strong enough to heal in place and don't feel the need to leave, that's fine too. It is your choice. There are resources in the back of this book to help you create a plan if you want to leave but are unsure how to get that done or where to go.

Children

If you have children and your partner (former or otherwise) is involved with them, I would encourage you to be respectful and make a huge effort not to be fearful, without being fake. If applicable, tell your child(ren) you don't hate their other parent, but staying together isn't healthy for you and you want them to be healthy too.

Your children will watch you. Your co-parent no longer gets to dictate your life and your child should see you setting boundaries and enforcing them. If your child sees you being spiteful and full of hate, that's how they will think they should be feeling. As much as that may please you, it is not a healthy place for your child to be. You can't control how your co-parent acts, but you can talk openly and honestly about what you see, and ask about your child's feelings as they move between the two of you. Let them know it is not their job to take care of their parents and help them rehearse how to set boundaries and say no.

That whole "it takes a village to raise a child" thing is real. Talk to your child's school staff and/or other adults in their lives. You shouldn't do this alone and neither should they. Normalize the fact that, in this family, we talk about our problems and we ask for help when we need it. I reached out to our school counselor to give a heads up about what was going on at home. Years later I found out that small task made a far greater impact on my children and my family than I will probably ever know.

Speaking of children, it would be good to step back and think about how you are parenting them. Are you allowing them to suffer the consequences of their own actions? Or are you taking those on as well? Are you protecting them from their own choices? Codependency is a way of life and tends to affect all of our close relationships. Continuously cleaning up their messes isn't helping you or them. Set healthy boundaries with your children. Allow them to make their own (age-appropriate) choices, and let them live with the consequences. If this is hard for you, remember that this is how they learn to make good decisions and to trust themselves.

And one more note on children... you do not have to be perfect for your kids. Kids need you to love them and accept them for who they are. A good way of modeling that is to expect them to accept you for Who You Are. You don't have to hide from them. You can have weaknesses. You don't want to make it scary or make them feel unsafe, but watching you heal will help them heal as well. Watching you set healthy boundaries will be a great example for them to use in their own lives.

Backsliding

There will be days when you hit a snag. It may be a flashback or nightmare; it may be seeing your partner or someone who looks like them or acts like them; it may be just a feeling or a thought that floats through. This is totally normal, so please don't panic. Your brain is an amazing processor, but it can only process to the capacity you have in the moment. You may process certain parts of a situation and think you have it, but later you will learn or feel something that makes you understand it on a completely different level, and it's okay to revisit your original stance or add to it. That is just your brain telling you it now has space or knowledge to do more.

It might be that you have moved out of fight-or-flight mode and are in a better place to think about the situation. As you get more distant from where you were, you are able to lay more thoughts to rest and ponder the next thing. Sometimes the next thing is a great revelation and makes your situation easier to understand and put into a new perspective.

Occasionally the new perspective takes you down a different road that requires going back to "the work" in Part II in order to push through it. Sometimes the thing that requires work is just the next one in line that your brain puts off until you are in a more stable place. Your brain does this for a reason. It is not "your fault" or some defect in your thinking that made you miss this different perspective. It was *by design*. Your brain protected you until you had the capacity to work through it.

That said, you still need to work through it. Go back to Part II, use the tools, and do the work. You will be amazed at how quickly you can get through these interruptions now that you understand where they come from, and have the tools to combat them. It always amazes me how the universe puts certain books or people in my path at just the right time to point me in a new, healing direction. Let's be honest, it's usually multiple people, a book, a podcast, and three articles. The universe is not subtle in my world.

Celebrate

Revisiting the bad relationship is hard. Figuring out the latest lesson to be learned can be frustrating. Using your tools to push through and find your truth again is a battle. Don't be too hard on yourself in the thick of it. Cut yourself some slack and live the best you can. Know that it is just another piece of the puzzle and you're getting that much closer to feeling whole.

I hit a spot a long time ago where I could not function. My thoughts just stopped. I was trying to carry on with my life and it was not having any of it. A wise person told me that doing the best I can isn't doing my best ever, it's doing the best I can in the situation I'm in right now, for today. The best I can do may just be getting out of bed today. That's okay. Whatever that situation is, it will pass and I will be able to do better later. Accepting yourself in the moment will help you get through it.

Give yourself credit for that best. (I got out of bed. I didn't want to, but I did it.) Keep trying. Give yourself credit when you win! This is not a small accomplishment. Making yourself vulnerable, allowing yourself to feel, exploring your feelings and taking steps to work through all of the factors that got you to this moment is a LOT. When you recognize a faulty belief, give yourself credit for the recognition. When you work through one of those lessons, take a moment to celebrate. You got this!

Going Above and Beyond

When you get to a point where you can look back at what happened in the relationship somewhat objectively, you may discover your partner really isn't that bad. Just as you had bad reactions to the changes in them, they had bad reactions to the changes in you. From that viewpoint, you may see things in their past that led them here, or you may come to understand that insecurity played a large role in the problem, and they may otherwise be a decent human. You may even recognize that if you had chosen not to heal, you may have taken their role in your next relationship. (Scary thought, isn't it?)

This is not to say that you have to trust them again. I am not saying that you have to accept any abuse you endured as normal. Maybe they really were that bad. Maybe they just aren't a decent human. Maybe there's a serious mental health issue that they aren't willing to address. That's not for me to judge. I want to make space for the possibility that whatever you saw in them to begin with is still there, and you didn't make such a terrible choice; you just missed the insecurity that brought the whole thing down.

If you are still in the relationship, or out of it and considering going back in, I'm not suggesting you should go back into it hoping your new tools will make it better. Hopefully by now you have a whole different way of approaching the relationship, but your partner does not. You can't expect the relationship to be healthy when only one half has healed. Your partner will need to do the work to root out the insecurity and learn the tools to have healthy relationships. Even then, it will take a long time for both of you to learn new habits and ways to communicate and build up trust. Old habits will reappear and you will both need to recognize them and remove them.

If you're going to try to rebuild the relationship, I recommend couples counseling to give you neutral space to work out new ways of arguing, expressing needs, and working through trust issues. It is a long road and not for the faint of heart. And again, you always have the option to leave.

If you are still in the relationship for children, safety, financial, building your self-esteem, or other reasons and your partner is unwilling to change, just keep building. Get strong, stay strong. Use your tools, keep working on yourself, and trust that the universe will open up an opportunity for you. Don't let your partner stop you from being Who You Are. You will recognize what you deserve and act on it when the time is right.

Chapter Twelve
What Does Moving On Look Like?

What does moving on look like to you? For me, it's being able to say no. It's being alone and not feeling lost or lonely. It's stating my opinion and not feeling like a burden. It's feeling comfortable in my own skin. It's knowing my own worth. It feels free. I don't need someone else to validate me or give me my worth. Moving on feels like being myself, only taking on the consequences of my own actions, having healthy boundaries and freedom to live without fear. I am whole.

That all sounds lovely, but life rarely feels that easy. There are still plenty of relationships in my life that I need to work on regularly. There are still people that I react to poorly out of habit. It helps to reframe them as capable people, able to handle their own consequences, but it also helps to tell myself their circumstances are not mine to handle. I don't need to know every detail of their lives so I can jump to the rescue. I can tolerate space. They can have their own lives and I can have mine, and we're all healthy humans. And when we come together, we can talk about what happened and how we felt about it, and we can let each other have our own feelings and respect them without having to fix them.

What happens when a new relationship comes along? How do you know you won't "do it again"?

Here's a thought: you don't need a romantic partner. You are a whole person and you are not more, nor less, whether you have a partner or not. The choice is entirely yours.

You may find someone who sees your truth and, because of that, be attracted to them. That's completely reasonable. In my experience, people who see my truth aren't necessarily good for me. Think about what a romantic relationship with this person would look like. Are they a whole person? Do they have codependent behaviors that would be triggering to you? Would it feel like your past?

The someone who sees your truth may be better as a business partner than a romantic partner. Perhaps they see your creative vision and they have the skills to make it work. Maybe they share your vision of how to make the world a better place. Whatever that truth looks like, you will still need to use the relationship skills you have to maintain that partnership, because codependency isn't only about romance. It is fundamental to your relationships, and you need to root it out of all of them.

You know what codependency and loss of yourself looks like. You know what it feels like. Now you have to trust yourself to know what you know. Listen to your inner voice. Listen to your body. Listen to your truth. You know what the old beliefs did to your self-esteem and your body will recognize that when it tries to come back.

For example, I have learned to identify shame. I know how it feels, where my thoughts go, and that there is always untruth in shame. Look for the untruth. Reject the old beliefs. I know those beliefs are where my shame is coming from, and I can choose to leave those unhealthy beliefs in the past.

You do the work, but when you enter a new relationship, triggers happen. It may be a smell or a sound that is connected to a memory and does not have anything to do with what actually happened in the current situation. Your partner needs to understand your past and provide:

- safety & security (In whatever way that looks like for you.)
- reassurance ("I have the option, but I am not leaving.")
- trust (You expect what happened before and you need to learn to trust that is not who they are. They need to be trustworthy.)

Can this person be those things to you? If so, are you willing to be honest with them and tell them about your past so they *can* understand? Someone who sees your truth still needs to be told the parts that weren't truthful to understand the full picture. You still have to use words. If you aren't ready or willing to use words, you should probably hold off on establishing a new relationship.

What does this look like in practice? You feel a trigger, something that makes you feel like you're not enough. The shameful thoughts start. You recognize the thoughts and you tell your partner about them and what triggered them (again using your words). They accept your feelings. They may apologize if something they did caused you to feel that way, they may use reassurance if it was something that made you feel abandoned, but in any case, they *listen* to you and react appropriately. They don't tell you it was your fault or belittle you. They only take responsibility for what is theirs to take. They don't try to give you more responsibility than what is yours. They don't tell you that you can't feel that way and they don't tell you what to feel. This is what not being codependent looks like.

Your job here is to first speak up about what you don't like or are uncomfortable with, then *hear* what they are saying, not what your past experience tells you to hear, and not to project any negative self-talk into what is actually being said. If you are not healthy enough to do these things most of the time, again, maybe hold off on starting a relationship until you are a little stronger. We all have our moments. I'm not saying you need to use all of the tools all of the time. You do need to be capable of being healthy for a relationship to work. Being healthy means being vulnerable enough to speak what you need, and being whole enough to accept love in return. Vulnerability requires strength and the belief that you are worth standing up for. You need to love yourself first.

Anybody can leave. As I've been saying throughout this book, you always have the option to leave the relationship. But also, so does your partner. If you're no longer good for each other, for whatever reason, it's okay to leave. As whole people you should be able to talk about the reasons, and if the reasons feel or sound lame, then dig into them and find the real ones. People screw up. You don't need to bail over the first thing. But if there's consistent behavior that makes one of the partners feel less than Who They Are, or other than Who They Are, then the conversation needs to happen. It's hard to break old habits. Circumstances change. Things happen.

If the two of you determine that there is no way to resolve the real reasons as whole people, then leaving is a natural action and you should both understand it. There doesn't need to be drama. There can be heartache; it's okay to grieve the loss. If you're not being whole people, then all the more reason to leave. If you have slipped back into codependency, then here's your reality check and it's time to actually face those demons. If you have continued to grow and you realize your partnership is no longer appropriate for whatever reason, then it's okay to choose yourself and allow yourself the space to keep growing. If your partner is in either of those positions then this is still not the best relationship for you. There are hosts of other reasons and the reason doesn't matter as much as choosing yourself and showing up for yourself. With that focus, you will be fine.

If you enter a relationship with the thought, "I am a whole person with my own thoughts, emotions, talents, hopes, dreams, and goals. If I want to be in a relationship, my significant other should see me as a whole person and should also be a whole person themselves." Then you need to give them space to also have their own thoughts, emotions, talents, hopes, dreams, and goals. Theirs, not yours. Theirs may be similar, but they don't have to be. If they like going fishing for hours on end and you find it boring, you don't need to go fishing. Their dreams may be the same, but with wildly different ways of getting there. Their being whole requires that you don't try to interfere with who they are. The two of you can debate tactics all day long, but you need to respect that their thoughts and opinions are valid. If you can't do that, you're probably in the wrong relationship.

You also need to allow them to make mistakes, and not only make the mistakes, but also clean up after themselves. Accept that they aren't going to be perfect, you're not perfect, mistakes will be made, and it is not the end of the world. It is actually a sign that your world is healthy. Hiding them or covering them up is still a codependent way of "cleaning up" and communicating that there is shame in it. Making a point to talk about the mistakes in a non-judgmental manner normalizes that they happen and there is no shame to be had there. Insulating your relationship from shame in this way is a great way to help it thrive.

The most important part of moving forward is knowing Who You Are. In order to stand firm in your relationships, you need to love yourself first. If you can look at these statements and feel like there's truth there, you are well on your way.

I am capable of having good relationships.
I am worthy of love.
I am enough and not "too much."
I have a vision for where I want to go.

That vision may be only for tomorrow; don't get too stressed about it. It expresses hope for the future. If you don't have them now, you will build larger visions as you build confidence in and explore your truth. Once you start to see yourself through this lens, you will grow and take up more space and naturally start looking further ahead. It is all part of becoming Who You Were

Meant to Be. And maybe you will feel the need to add another belief to your list:

10. *I will not betray who I am.*

Part IV: Resources

Much of this book is my lived experience. It incorporates advice from friends, health care providers, years of therapy, training, thoughts from books I've read, podcasts, articles, blogs, music, movies, videos, memes, social media, overheard conversations, you name it. My mind is a strange and wonderful place that tends to merge new thoughts into my big picture very quickly. For that reason, I don't have a ton of exact references in this book other than words I specifically looked up to quote for clarity. However, these are resources that I would recommend for digging deeper into some of the things I've talked about.

<u>Resources List:</u>

The Anatomy of Anxiety: Understanding and Overcoming the Body's Fear Response by Ellen Vora, M.D.
I stumbled upon her book toward the end of writing this book. Super helpful if you deal with anxiety in any of its many manifestations.

Atlas of the Heart: Mapping Meaningful Connection and the Language of Human Experience by Brené Brown, Ph.D., MSW

Really, just read anything by Brené. I like the groupings of emotions in this specific book because it speaks to where emotions come from.

The Body Keeps the Score: Brain, Mind, and Body in the Healing of Trauma by Bessel van der Kolk, M.D.
A psychiatrist's guide to the physical effects of trauma on the body. The first half can get pretty heavy. If it bogs you down, skip to the second half, which is a very helpful list of alternative treatments for people who haven't responded well to traditional mental health treatments.

The Book of Boundaries: Set the Limits That Will Set You Free by Melissa Urban
Very practical guide to how boundaries work with a multitude of real-life examples on how to use them.

Codependent No More: How to Stop Controlling Others and Start Caring for Yourself by Melody Beattie
This book goes in-depth on codependency. As far as I know, my codependency doesn't have anything to do with alcohol or other substance use disorders, but if yours does, this book covers that. It also contains activities after each chapter that encourage you to really stop and think and apply what you just read. If you are having problems coming up with your list of beliefs, this book may help you take a deeper look at yourself.

DEI Training—led by Dr. Leeno Karumanchery, Sociologist and Co-Founder of MESH/ diversity. www.meshdiversity.com

I did this training for work and I want to give it credit for helping me find words around societal oppression of women and others.

Trauma-Informed Yoga: A Toolbox for Therapists: 47 Simple Practices to Calm, Balance, and Restore the Nervous System by Joanne Spence, MA, E-RYT 500, C-IAYT
To be honest, I didn't want to read heavy psychological texts on polyvagal theory so I chose a book that summarizes and puts it into practice. It did what I needed. It also has some yoga practices that are very helpful.

Untamed by Glennon Doyle
Celebrates the act of choosing yourself. The dedication says, "For every woman resurrecting herself." When you need some motivation, this book will give you a boost.

Glennon Doyle's podcast *We Can Do Hard Things* episodes #86, 87 and 120 with Jen Hatmaker
Inspired me to understand that I'm not the only one.

Whole Brain Living: The Anatomy of Choice and the Four Characters That Drive Our Life by Jill Bolte Taylor, Ph.D.
I am a brain geek and this book is a fascinating read about how the brain works. I suggest watching her TED talk first to give you an idea of where she is coming from.

Resources for Leaving a Relationship
(mentioned in Chapter 11)

National Domestic Violence Hotline

https://www.thehotline.org/

This site is the one place to go if you are looking to leave an abusive relationship. They have call, chat and text options if you want to talk to someone. The "Get Help" section points you to local resources. There are lots of resources if you are just looking for information and not yet ready to act. Using a computer at a public library to download information, or using a friend's device will help keep your plans private.

"Leaving an Abusive Relationship," U.S. Department of Health & Human Services, The Office on Women's Health, accessed November 26, 2023.

https://www.womenshealth.gov/relationships-and-safety/domestic-violence/leaving-abusive-relationship

This site provides a Q&A style list of helpful information, reprinted below. It ultimately recommends the National Domestic Violence Hotline, above.

- **Identify a safe friend or friends and safe places to go.** Create a code word to use with friends, family, or neighbors to let them know you are in danger without the abuser finding out. If possible, agree on a secret location where they can pick you up.
- **Keep an alternate cellphone nearby.** Try not to call for help on your home phone or on a shared cellphone. Your partner might be able to trace the numbers. If

you don't have a cellphone, you can get a prepaid cellphone. Some domestic violence shelters offer free cellphones.

- **Memorize the phone numbers of friends, family, or shelters.** If your partner takes your phone, you will still be able to contact loved ones or shelters for a safe place to stay.

- **Make a list of things to take if you have to leave quickly.** Important identity documents and money are probably the top priority. See the Safety Packing List for a detailed list of items to pack. Get these items together, and keep them in a safe place where your partner will not find them. If you are in immediate danger, leave without them.

- **If you can, hide an extra set of car keys** so you can leave if your partner takes away your usual keys.

- **Ask your doctor how to get extra medicine or glasses, hearing aids, or other medically necessary items for you or your children.**

- **Contact your local family court** (or domestic violence court, if your state has one) for information about getting a restraining order. If you need legal help but don't have much money, your local domestic violence agency may be able to help you find a lawyer who will work for free or on a sliding scale based on what you can pay.

- **Protect your online security** as you collect information and prepare. Use a computer at a public library to download information, or use a friend's computer or cellphone. Your partner might be able to track your planning otherwise.

- **Try to take with you any evidence of abuse or violence** if you leave your partner. This might include threatening notes from your partner. It might be copies of police and medical reports. It might include pictures of your injuries or damage to your property.
- **Keep copies of all paper and electronic documents on an external thumb drive.**

Acknowledgements

I would like to thank my alpha and beta readers, Angela, Kyle, Tiffany, Laura, Lynn, Tim, Beth, Shelley, Rose, Sam, Heather, Deb, and Beth. Your input made this book become what it was supposed to be. You volunteered! You kept dragging me back when I strayed from the path and gave me encouragement when my motivation waned. Know that every little thing made a difference.

Thanks also to my editors, Carol Shay Hornung and Kathy Hayevsky. You provided two completely different sets of skills I lack and the perspective I needed to step back and see things from a new angle. You are just what I needed! Carol, many thanks for the author tips and sharing your knowledge of writing, editing and publishing. I had no idea what I was getting into.

Thanks to my proofreader, Veronica Hoffman. You are a true professional and made it easy to trust you with the final polish.

Thanks for artistic advice to Thom Gravelle. You went above and beyond with your formatting flair. Thanks also to Julie, Tiff and Angela. Thank you for being supportive of my vision, and for giving me your honest feedback on all the iterations.

Thank you to Shelley for allowing me to live in your cabin in the woods for four weeks while I was writing. That was truly inspiring.

Thank you to Grant for asking why.

Thank you to Angela for continuously asking my advice, and for clearly explaining why you needed it.

Thank you to Holly, for repeatedly telling me I can leave.

Thank you to the multiple public libraries that gave me a quiet, neutral space to work and access to research all the things that go into a book.

About the Author

Barbara Leigh grew up on a dairy farm in Wisconsin and spent most of her developing years well liked, but never quite fitting in. She went off to college where she found some of her best friends and also some of her worst relationships. She carried those bad relationships into her marriage, career and family until one day she decided to just stop. She has spent the last twenty years figuring out what it means to stop, how to continue living, and how to do it better.

Read the afterword at www.barbaraleighauthor.com/afterword.

www.ingramcontent.com/pod-product-compliance
Lightning Source LLC
Chambersburg PA
CBHW032056040426
42335CB00036B/409